Jefferson Davis and his Cabinet

Biographies of Great Statesmen

Editor: Joe Mieczkowski, Gettysburg Licensed Battlefield Guide

Title: Jefferson Davis and his Cabinet

Subtitle: Biographies of Great Statesmen

Editor: Joe Mieczkowski, Gettysburg Licensed Battlefield Guide

Created on: 2013-07-09 10:19 (CET)

ISBN: 978-3868980011

Produced by: PediaPress GmbH, Taunusstrasse 61, Mainz, Germany, http://pediapress.com/

The content within this book was generated collaboratively by volunteers. Please be advised that nothing found here has necessarily been reviewed by people with the expertise required to provide you with complete, accurate or reliable information. Some information in this book may be misleading or simply wrong. PediaPress does not guarantee the validity of the information found here. If you need specific advice (for example, medical, legal, financial, or risk management) please seek a professional who is licensed or knowledgeable in that area.

Sources, licenses and contributors of the articles and images are listed in the section entitled "References". Parts of the books may be licensed under the GNU Free Documentation License. A copy of this license is included in the section entitled "GNU Free Documentation License"

All third-party trademarks used belong to their respective owners.

Create your own custom Wikipedia-Book at http://pediapress.com

collection id:
pdf writer version: 0.10.1 mwlib version: 0.15.8

Contents

Articles	**1**
Preface	1
President	**3**
Jefferson Davis	3
President of the Provisional Confederate Congress	**25**
Howell Cobb	25
Vice President	**33**
Alexander H. Stephens	33
Secretary of State: Toombs, Hunter, Benjamin*	**43**
Robert Toombs	43
Robert M. T. Hunter	50
Secretary of War :Walker, Benjamin*, Randolph, Seddon, Breckinridge	**55**
LeRoy Pope Walker	55
George W. Randolph	58
James Seddon	61
John C. Breckinridge	63
Secretary of the Treasury:Memminger, Trenholm, Reagan**	**73**
Christopher Memminger	73
George Trenholm	77

Attorney General   79

    Judah P. Benjamin 79

    Thomas Bragg 89

    Thomas H. Watts 91

    George Davis (politician) 93

Postmaster General   97

    John Henninger Reagan 97

Secretary of the Navy   105

    Stephen Mallory 105

* Judah Benjamin held 3 posts: Attorney General, War and State   121

** John Reagan held 2 posts: Postmaster General and Treasury   123

Appendix   125

    References 125

    Article Sources and Contributors 134

    Image Sources, Licenses and Contributors 136

Article Licenses   139

Index   141

Preface

Since the Confederacy was founded on states' rights, one important factor in Jefferson Davis' choice of cabinet members was representation from the various states. He depended partly upon recommendations from congressmen and other prominent people, and this helped maintain good relations between the executive and legislative branches. As more states joined the Confederacy, though, this also led to complaints when there were more states than cabinet positions. Once the war began, there were frequent changes to the cabinet.

Joe Mieczkowski is a Civil War living historian and educator. Having received his Bachelor's Degree from Salem College and his Master's Degree in Public Administration from Pennsylvania State University, Joe's education provided the foundation to support his 37 year career with the Social Security Administration. He served in a variety of locations and positions, including 16 years as a Manager and Area Director in Washington, D.C. and he retired from federal service as the Area Director in Harrisburg, PA. Joe is an Adjunct Professor for local community colleges, teaching courses in various aspects of American History. In addition, Joe teaches management and leadership courses including project management and executive development. As a leadership training consultant, Joe works with numerous educational, governmental, and corporate organizations. He is a Licensed Battlefield and Town Guide for the Gettysburg National Military Park, and is a Past President of the Gettysburg Civil War Roundtable.

Joe is a resident of Fairfield, PA, where he lives with his wife, Chris.

President

Jefferson Davis

	Jefferson Davis
	President of the Confederate States of America
	In office February 18, 1861 - May 5, 1865
Vice President	Alexander Stephens
Preceded by	*Office instituted*
Succeeded by	*Office abolished*
	23rd United States Secretary of War
	In office March 7, 1853 - March 3, 1857
President	Franklin Pierce
Preceded by	Charles Magill Conrad
Succeeded by	John Buchanan Floyd
	United States Senator from Mississippi

	In office August 10, 1847 - September 23, 1851
Preceded by	Jesse Speight
Succeeded by	John J. McRae
	In office March 4, 1857 - January 21, 1861[1]
Preceded by	Stephen Adams
Succeeded by	Adelbert Ames (1870)

Member of the U.S. House of Representatives from Mississippi's At-large district	
	In office December 8, 1845 - June 1, 1846
Preceded by	Tilghman M. Tucker
Succeeded by	Henry T. Ellett
Personal details	
Born	June 3, 1808 Christian County, Kentucky
Died	December 6, 1889 (aged 81) New Orleans, Louisiana
Citizenship	Confederate
Nationality	American
Political party	Democratic
Spouse(s)	Sarah Knox Taylor Varina Howell
Alma mater	Jefferson College Transylvania University United States Military Academy
Profession	Soldier, Politician
Religion	Episcopal
Signature	*Jefferson Davis*
Military service	
Allegiance	Confederate States of America United States of America
Service/branch	United States Army Mississippi Rifles
Years of service	1828-1835, 1846-1847
Rank	Colonel
Battles/wars	Mexican-American War

Jefferson Finis Davis (June 3, 1808 - December 6, 1889), also known as

Jeff Davis, was an American statesman and leader of the Confederacy during the American Civil War, serving as President for its entire history. He was born in Kentucky to Samuel and Jane (Cook) Davis. After attending Transylvania University, Davis graduated from West Point and fought in the Mexican-American War as a colonel of a volunteer regiment. He served as the United States Secretary of War under Democratic President Franklin Pierce. Both before and after his time in the Pierce administration, he served as a Democratic U.S. Senator representing the State of Mississippi. As a senator, he argued against secession, but did agree that each state was sovereign and had an unquestionable right to secede from the Union.[2]

On February 9, 1861, after he resigned from the United States Senate, Davis was selected to be the provisional President of the Confederate States of America; he was elected without opposition to a six-year term that November. During his presidency, Davis took charge of the Confederate war plans but was unable to find a strategy to stop the larger, more powerful and better organized Union. His diplomatic efforts failed to gain recognition from any foreign country, and he paid little attention to the collapsing Confederate economy, printing more and more paper money to cover the war's expenses. Historians have criticized Davis for being a much less effective war leader than his Union counterpart Abraham Lincoln, which they attribute to Davis being overbearing, controlling, and overly meddlesome, as well as being out of touch with public opinion, and lacking support from a political party (since the Confederacy had no political parties).[3] His preoccupation with detail, reluctance to delegate responsibility, lack of popular appeal, feuds with powerful state governors, inability to get along with people who disagreed with him, neglect of civil matters in favor of military ones—all these shortcomings worked against him.[4]

After Davis was captured on May 10, 1865, he was charged with treason. Although he was not tried, he was stripped of his eligibility to run for public office; Congress posthumously lifted this restriction in 1978.[5] While not disgraced, he was displaced in Southern affection after the war by the leading Confederate general Robert E. Lee. However, many Southerners empathized with his defiance, refusal to accept defeat, and resistance to Reconstruction. Over time, admiration for his pride and ideals made him a Civil War hero to many Southerners, and his legacy became part of the foundation of the postwar New South.[6] In spite of his former status as the president of the Confederacy, Jefferson Davis began to encourage reconciliation by the late 1880s, telling Southerners to be loyal to the Union.[7,8,9]

Early life and first military career

Davis' grandfather, Evan Davies, was born in Philadelphia in 1702; his father or grandfather had emigrated to North America from Wales. Evan married Lydia Emory Williams, also from Philadelphia. Samuel Emory Davis was born to them in 1756. Lydia had two sons from a previous marriage; along with his two half-brothers, Samuel served in the Continental Army during the American Revolutionary War. He later married Jane Cook, who was born in Christian County, Kentucky in 1759 to William Cook and his wife Sarah Simpson. Samuel and Jane were married in 1783 and had 10 children. Jefferson was the last and was born on June 3, 1808. Samuel died on July 4, 1824, and Jane on October 3, 1845.[10]

During Davis' youth, his family moved twice: in 1811 to St. Mary Parish, Louisiana and in 1812 to Wilkinson County, Mississippi. Three of Jefferson's older brothers served during the War of 1812. In 1813 Davis began his education at the Wilkinson Academy, near the family plantation in the small town of Woodville. Two years later, Davis entered the Catholic school of Saint Thomas at St. Rose Priory, a school operated by the Dominican Order in Washington County, Kentucky. At the time, he was the only Protestant student at the school. Davis went on to Jefferson College at Washington, Mississippi in 1818, and then to Transylvania University at Lexington, Kentucky in 1821.[11]

In 1824 Davis entered the United States Military Academy (West Point).[12] While at West Point, Davis was placed under house arrest for his role in the Eggnog Riot in Christmas 1826, but graduated 23rd in a class of 33 in June 1828.[13] Following graduation, Second Lieutenant Davis was assigned to the 1st Infantry Regiment and was stationed at Fort Crawford, Wisconsin. Lt. Davis was home in Mississippi for the entire Black Hawk War of 1832, but was assigned by his colonel, Zachary Taylor, to escort Black Hawk himself to prison. It is said that the chief liked Davis because of the kind treatment he had shown.[14]

Marriage, plantation life, and early political career

Davis served under Zachary Taylor starting in 1832. That same year, Taylor's family, including his daughter Sarah Knox Taylor, joined him at Fort Crawford, and Jefferson and Sarah became friends and fell in love. At first her father had nothing against Davis personally, but he did not want Sarah to be an army wife, having had first-hand experience with the combination of family and military life. Later, Taylor developed a dislike for Davis, but the couple continued to see each other and intended to marry. When Davis left Fort Crawford in

Figure 1: *First wife, Sarah Knox Taylor*

1833, he did not see Sarah for over two years. During this time he decided to leave the army and become a cotton planter with his brother Joseph; this may have been partly due to Zachary Taylor's concerns. Sarah and Jefferson were married on June 17, 1835, at the house of her aunt near Louisville, Kentucky. The newly weds settled at the groom's brother Joseph Davis' plantation at Davis Bend in Warren County, Mississippi, but the marriage proved to be short. While visiting Davis' oldest sister near Saint Francisville, Louisiana, both newlyweds contracted malaria, and Sarah died three months after the wedding on September 15, 1835.[12,15]

Joseph gave his brother 900 acres of land adjoining his property where Davis built Brierfield Plantation. At the time Davis had only one slave, James Pemberton. Clearing the land and growing cotton required slave labor and by early 1836 Davis had purchased 16 slaves. The number increased to 40 by 1840 and 74 by 1845. Pemberton served as Davis' overseer, an unusual position for a slave in Mississippi.[16]

For the next eight years, Davis was reclusive, studying government and history and engaging in private political discussions with his brother Joseph. In 1840 he attended a Democratic meeting in Vicksburg and, to his surprise, was chosen as a delegate to the party's state convention in Jackson. In 1842 he once again attended the Democratic convention, and in 1843 became a candidate

Figure 2: *Second wife, Varina Howell*

for the state House of Representatives but lost his first election. The following year, 1844, Davis was sent to the party convention for a third time and his interest in politics deepened. He was selected as one of six presidential electors for the 1844 presidential election and campaigned effectively throughout Mississippi for the Democratic candidate, James K. Polk[17,18]

That same year, Davis met Varina Howell, the granddaughter of the late New Jersey Governor Richard Howell. Within a month of their meeting, Davis had asked her to marry him. They married on February 26, 1845. His political activity continued. On July 8, 1845 he received the party's nomination for one of the at-large seats in United States House of Representatives and in November he was elected. He was sworn into office on December 8, 1845.[19]

Jefferson and Varina Howell Davis had six children; three died before reaching adulthood. Their first son, Samuel Emory, was born July 30, 1852, and was named after his grandfather; he died June 30, 1854, of an undiagnosed disease at less than two years old.[20] Margaret Howell was born the following year on February 25, 1855.[21] She married Joel Addison Hayes Junior (1848-1919) and moved to Colorado Springs. They had five children; Margaret was the only child of Jefferson and Varina to marry and raise a family. She died on July 18, 1909 at the age of 54.[22]

Figure 3: *Daughter Winnie Davis*

Their third child, Jefferson Davis Junior, was born on January 16, 1857. He died of yellow fever at age 21 on October 16, 1878, during an epidemic that swept the Mississippi river valley and claimed the lives of 20,000 people.[23] Joseph Evan was born on April 18, 1859, and died at five years old as the result of an accidental fall on April 30, 1864.[24] William Howell was born on December 6, 1861, and died of diphtheria on October 16, 1872, before reaching the age of 11.[25] Varina Anne "Winnie" Davis was born on June 27, 1864, several months after Joseph's death. She died on September 18, 1898, at age 34.[26]

Second military career

In 1846 the Mexican-American War began. Davis resigned his house seat in June and raised a volunteer regiment, the Mississippi Rifles, becoming its colonel.[27] On July 21, 1846, they sailed from New Orleans for the Texas coast. Davis armed the regiment with the M1841 Mississippi Rifle and trained the regiment in its use, making it particularly effective in combat.[28] In September 1846 Davis participated in the successful siege of Monterrey.[29]

On February 22, 1847, Davis fought bravely at the Battle of Buena Vista and was shot in the foot, being carried to safety by Robert H. Chilton. In recognition of Davis' bravery and initiative, commanding general Zachary Taylor is reputed to have said, "My daughter, sir, was a better judge of men than I was."[12] On May 17, 1847, President James K. Polk offered Davis a Federal commission as a brigadier general and command of a brigade of militia. Davis declined the appointment arguing that the United States Constitution gives the power of appointing militia officers to the states, and not to the Federal government of the United States.[30]

Return to politics

Senator

Because of his war service, Governor Brown of Mississippi appointed Davis to fill out the senate term of the late Jesse Speight. He took his seat on December 5, 1847, and was elected to serve the remainder of his term in January 1848.[31] The Smithsonian Institution appointed him a regent at the end of December 1847.[32]

In 1848 Senator Davis introduced the first of several proposed amendments to the Treaty of Guadalupe Hidalgo; this one would annex most of northeastern Mexico and failed with a vote of 44 to 11.[33] Regarding Cuba, Davis declared that it "must be ours" to "increase the number of slaveholding constituencies."[34] He also was concerned about the security implications of a Spanish holding lying a few miles off the coast of Florida.[35]

A group of Cuban revolutionaries led by Narciso López intended to forcibly liberate Cuba from Spanish rule. In 1849, López visited Davis and asked him to lead his filibuster expedition to Cuba. He offered an immediate payment of $100,000,[36] plus the same amount when Cuba was liberated. Davis turned down the offer, stating that it was inconsistent with his duty as a senator. When asked to recommend someone else, Davis suggested Robert E. Lee, then an army major in Baltimore; López approached Lee, who also declined on the grounds of his duty.[37,38]

The senate made Davis chairman of the Committee on Military Affairs. When his term expired he was elected to the same seat (by the Mississippi legislature, as the constitution mandated at the time). He had not served a year when he resigned (in September 1851) to run for the governorship of Mississippi on the issue of the Compromise of 1850, which Davis opposed. He was defeated by fellow Senator Henry Stuart Foote by 999 votes.[39] Left without political office, Davis continued his political activity. He took part in a convention on states' rights, held at Jackson, Mississippi, in January 1852. In the weeks leading up to the presidential election of 1852, he campaigned in numerous Southern states for Democratic candidates Franklin Pierce and William R. King.[40]

Secretary of War

Franklin Pierce won the presidential election, and in 1853 he made Davis his Secretary of War.[41] In this capacity, Davis gave Congress four annual reports (in December of each year), as well as an elaborate one (submitted on February 22, 1855) on various routes for the proposed Transcontinental Railroad. He promoted the Gadsden Purchase of today's southern Arizona from Mexico. He also increased the size of the regular army from 11,000 to 15,000 and introduced general usage of the improved guns which he had used successfully during the Mexican-American War.[42]

The Pierce administration ended in 1857 with the loss of the Democratic nomination to James Buchanan. Davis' term was to end with Pierce's, so he ran successfully for the Senate, and re-entered it on March 4, 1857.[43]

Return to Senate

His renewed service in the senate was interrupted by an illness that threatened him with the loss of his left eye. Still nominally serving in the senate, Davis spent the summer of 1858 in Portland, Maine. On the Fourth of July, he delivered an anti-secessionist speech on board a ship near Boston. He again urged the preservation of the Union on October 11 in Faneuil Hall, Boston, and returned to the senate soon after.[44]

As Davis explained in his memoir *The Rise and Fall of the Confederate Government*, he believed that each state was sovereign and had an unquestionable right to secede from the Union. He counseled delay among his fellow Southerners, because he did not think that the North would permit the peaceable exercise of the right to secession. Having served as secretary of war under President Franklin Pierce, he also knew that the South lacked the military and naval resources necessary to defend itself if war were to break out. Following the election of Abraham Lincoln in 1860, however, events accelerated. South Carolina adopted an ordinance of secession on December 20, 1860, and Mississippi did so on January 9, 1861. Davis had expected this but waited until he received official notification; then on January 21, the day Davis called "the saddest day of my life",[45] he delivered a farewell address to the United States Senate, resigned and returned to Mississippi.[46]

President of the Confederate States of America

Anticipating a call for his services since Mississippi had seceded, Davis had sent a telegraph message to Governor Pettus saying, "Judge what Mississippi requires of me and place me accordingly."[47] On January 23, 1861, Pettus made Davis a major general of the Army of Mississippi.[12] On February 9, a

Figure 4: *Jefferson Davis is sworn in as President of the Confederate States of America on February 18, 1861, on the steps of the Alabama State Capitol.*

Figure 5: *The first Confederate postage stamp (1861)*

constitutional convention at Montgomery, Alabama, considered Davis, Howell Cobb, Alexander Stephens, and Robert Toombs for the office of provisional president. Davis was unanimously elected and was inaugurated on February 18, 1861.[48,49] He was chosen partly because he was a well-known and experienced moderate who had served in a president's cabinet. In meetings of his own Mississippi legislature, Davis had argued against secession; but when a majority of the delegates opposed him, he gave in.[50] Davis wanted to serve as a general in the Confederate States Army and not as the president, but accepted the role for which he had been chosen.[51]

Several forts in Confederate territory remained in Union hands. Davis sent a commission to Washington with an offer to pay for any Federal property on Southern soil, as well as the Southern portion of the national debt. Lincoln refused to meet it. Informal discussions did take place with Secretary of State William Seward through Supreme Court Justice John A. Campbell, an Alabamian who had not yet resigned; Seward hinted that Fort Sumter would be evacuated, but nothing definite was said.[52]

On March 1, Davis appointed General P. G. T. Beauregard to command all Confederate troops in the vicinity of Charleston, South Carolina, where state officials chafed to take possession of Fort Sumter; Beauregard was to prepare his forces but avoid an attack on the fort. When Lincoln moved to resupply the fort, Davis and his cabinet directed Beauregard to demand its surrender or else take possession by force. Major Anderson did not surrender, Beauregard bombarded the fort, and the Civil War began.[53]

When Virginia joined the Confederacy, Davis moved his government to Richmond in May 1861. He and his family took up his residence there at the White House of the Confederacy later that month.[54] Having served since February as the provisional president, Davis was elected to a full six-year term on November 6, 1861 and was inaugurated on February 22, 1862.[55]

In June 1862, in his most successful move, Davis assigned General Robert E. Lee to replace the wounded Joseph E. Johnston in command of the Army of Northern Virginia, the main Confederate army in the Eastern Theater. That December he made a tour of Confederate armies in the west of the country. Davis largely made the main strategic decisions on his own, or approved those suggested by Lee. He had a very small circle of military advisers. Davis evaluated the Confederacy's national resources and weaknesses and decided that in order to win its independence the Confederacy was going to have to fight mostly on the strategic defensive. Davis maintained mostly a defensive outlook throughout the war, paying special attention to the defense of his national capital at Richmond. He attempted strategic offensives when he felt that military

Figure 6: *The original Confederate Cabinet. L-R: Judah P. Benjamin, Stephen Mallory, Christopher Memminger, Alexander Stephens, LeRoy Pope Walker, Jefferson Davis, John H. Reagan and Robert Toombs*

success would shake Northern self-confidence and strengthen the peace movements there. The campaigns met defeat at Antietam (1862) and Gettysburg (1863).[56]

Administration and Cabinet

Since the Confederacy was founded on states' rights, one important factor in Davis' choice of cabinet members was representation from the various states. He depended partly upon recommendations from congressmen and other prominent people, and this helped maintain good relations between the executive and legislative branches. As more states joined the Confederacy, though, this also led to complaints when there were more states than cabinet positions.[57]

When Davis became the provisional president in 1861, he formed his first cabinet. Robert Toombs of Georgia was the first Secretary of State, and Christopher Memminger of South Carolina became Secretary of the Treasury. LeRoy Pope Walker of Alabama was made Secretary of War after being recommended for this post by Clement Clay and William Yancey (both of whom declined to accept cabinet positions themselves). John Reagan of Texas became Postmaster General, and Judah P. Benjamin of Louisiana became Attorney General. Although Stephen Mallory was not put forward by the delegation from his state of Florida, Davis insisted that he was the best man for the job of Secretary of the Navy, and he was eventually confirmed.[58]

Once the war began, there were frequent changes to the cabinet. Robert Hunter of Virginia replaced Toombs as Secretary of State on July 25, 1861. On September 17 Walker resigned as Secretary of War; Benjamin left the Attorney General position to take his place, and Thomas Bragg of North Carolina (brother of General Braxton Bragg) took Benjamin's place.[59]

Following the November 1861 election, Davis did not announce the permanent government's cabinet until March 1862. Benjamin moved again, to Secretary of State; George W. Randolph of Virginia had been made the Secretary of War. Mallory continued as Secretary of the Navy and Reagan as Postmaster General; both men kept their positions throughout the war. Memminger was still Secretary of the Treasury, while Thomas Hill Watts of Alabama was made Attorney General.[60]

In 1862, Randolph resigned from the War Department, and James Seddon of Virginia was appointed to replace him. In late 1863, Watts resigned as Attorney General to take office as the Governor of Alabama, and George Davis of North Carolina took his place. In 1864, Memminger withdrew from the treasury post due to opposition from the congress and was replaced by George Trenholm of South Carolina. In 1865, congressional opposition likewise caused Seddon to withdraw, and he was replaced by John C. Breckinridge of Kentucky.[61]

Strategic failures

Most historians sharply criticize Davis for his flawed military strategy, his selection of friends for military commands, and his neglect of the homefront crises.[62,63] Until late in the war he resisted efforts to appoint a general-in-chief, essentially handling those duties himself. On January 31, 1865, Lee assumed this role, but it was far too late. Davis insisted on a strategy of trying to defend all Southern territory with ostensibly equal effort, which diluted the limited resources of the South and made it vulnerable to coordinated strategic thrusts by the Union into the vital Western Theater, such as the capture of New Orleans in early 1862. He made other controversial strategic choices, such as allowing Lee to invade the North in 1862 and 1863 while the Western armies were under very heavy pressure. Not only did Lee lose at Gettysburg but simultaneously Vicksburg fell and the Union took control of the Mississippi River, splitting the Confederacy. At Vicksburg, the failure to coordinate multiple forces on both sides of the Mississippi River rested primarily on the inability of Davis to create a harmonious departmental arrangement or to force such commanders as generals Edmund Kirby Smith, Earl Van Dorn, and Theophilus H. Holmes to work together.[64]

Davis has been faulted for poor coordination and management of his generals. This includes his reluctance to relieve his personal friend, Braxton Bragg, defeated in important battles and distrusted by his subordinates. He did relieve the cautious but capable Joseph E. Johnston and replaced him with the reckless John Bell Hood, resulting in the loss of Atlanta and the eventual loss of an army.[65]

Davis gave speeches to soldiers and politicians but largely ignored the common people and thereby failed to harness Confederate nationalism by directing the energies of the people into winning the war. More and more, the plain folk resented the favoritism shown the rich and powerful.[66] Davis did not use his presidential pulpit to rally the people with stirring rhetoric—he called instead for people to be fatalistic and to die for their new country.[67] Apart from two month-long trips across the country where he met a few hundred people, Davis stayed in Richmond where few people saw him; newspapers had limited circulation and most Confederates had little favorable information about him.[68] In April 1863, food shortages led to rioting in Richmond, as poor people robbed and looted numerous stores for food until Davis cracked down and restored order.[69] Davis feuded bitterly with his vice president. Perhaps even more serious, he clashed with powerful state governors who used states' rights arguments to withhold their militia units from national service and otherwise blocked mobilization plans.[70]

Final days of the Confederacy

On April 3, 1865, with Union troops under Ulysses S. Grant poised to capture Richmond, Davis escaped for Danville, Virginia, together with the Confederate Cabinet, leaving on the Richmond and Danville Railroad. Lincoln sat in his Richmond office 40 hours after Davis' departure. On about April 12, he received Robert E. Lee's letter announcing surrender.[71] Davis issued his last official proclamation as president of the Confederacy, and then went south to Greensboro, North Carolina.[72]

After Lee's surrender, there was a public meeting in Shreveport, Louisiana, at which many speakers supported continuation of the war. Plans were developed for the Davis government to flee to Havana, Cuba. There, the leaders would regroup and head to the Confederate-controlled Trans-Mississippi area by way of the Rio Grande.[73] None of these plans was put into practice.

President Jefferson Davis met with his Confederate Cabinet for the last time on May 5, 1865, in Washington, Georgia, and the Confederate government was officially dissolved. The meeting took place at the Heard house, the Georgia Branch Bank Building, with 14 officials present. Along with a hand-picked escort led by Given Campbell, Davis was captured on May 10, 1865, at Irwinville in Irwin County, Georgia.[74] In the confusion, Davis put his wife's

Figure 7: *William T. Sutherlin Mansion, Danville, Virginia, temporary residence of Jefferson Davis and dubbed Last Capitol of the Confederacy*

overcoat over his shoulders and attempted to flee the Union soldiers, leading to caricatures of him being captured while disguised as a woman.[75] Meanwhile, Davis' belongings continued on the train bound for Cedar Key, Florida. They were first hidden at Senator David Levy Yulee's plantation in Florida, then placed in the care of a railroad agent in Waldo. On June 15, 1865, Union soldiers seized Davis' personal baggage, together with some of the Confederate government's records, from the agent. A historical marker now stands at this site.[76,77,78]

Imprisonment and later years

On May 19, 1865, Davis was imprisoned in a casemate at Fortress Monroe, on the coast of Virginia. He was placed in irons for three days. Davis was indicted for treason a year later. While in prison, Davis arranged to sell his Mississippi estate to one of his former slaves, Ben Montgomery. While he was in prison, Pope Pius IX sent Davis a portrait of himself on which were written the Latin words "Venite ad me omnes qui laboratis, et ego reficiam vos, dicit Dominus", which comes from Matthew 11:28 and translates as, "Come to me all ye who labor and are heavy burdened and I will give you rest, sayeth the Lord." A hand-woven crown of thorns associated with the portrait is often said

Figure 8: *Contemporary sketch of Davis imprisoned in Ft. Monroe*

to have been made by the Pope himself,[79] but in fact it may have woven by Varina Davis.[80]

After two years of imprisonment, he was released on bail of $100,000 which was posted by prominent citizens of both Northern and Southern states, including Horace Greeley, Cornelius Vanderbilt and Gerrit Smith (a former member of the Secret Six who had supported John Brown). Davis visited Canada, Cuba and Europe. In December 1868 the court rejected a motion to nullify the indictment, but the prosecution dropped the case in February 1869. That same year, Davis became president of the Carolina Life Insurance Company in Memphis, Tennessee. He turned down the opportunity to become the first president of the Agricultural and Mechanical College of Texas (now Texas A&M University).[81]

During Reconstruction, Davis remained silent; however, he privately expressed opinions that federal military rule and Republican authority over former Confederate states was unjustified. He considered "Yankee and Negroe" rule in the south oppressive. Davis held contemporary beliefs that African Americans were inferior to the white race. Historian William J. Cooper stated that Davis believed in southern social order that included "a democratic white polity based firmly on dominance of a controlled and excluded black caste."[82] In 1876, Davis promoted a society for the stimulation of U.S. trade with South America. He visited England the next year, returning in 1878 to Beauvoir.

Figure 9:
Jefferson Davis at his home c.1885

Over the next three years there, Davis wrote *The Rise and Fall of the Confederate Government*.[83]

Davis' reputation in the South was restored by the book and by his warm reception on his tour of the region in 1886 and 1887. In numerous stops he attended "Lost Cause" ceremonies, where large crowds showered him with affection and local leaders presented emotional speeches honoring his sacrifices to the would-be nation. The *Meriden Daily Journal* stated that Davis, at a reception held in New Orleans in May, 1887, urged southerners to be loyal to the nation. He said, "United you are now, and if the Union is ever to be broken, let the other side break it." Davis stated that men in the Confederacy had successfully fought for their own rights with inferior numbers during the Civil War and that the northern historians ignored this view.[8] Davis, however, firmly believed that Confederate secession was constitutional. The former Confederate president was optimistic concerning American prosperity and the next generation.[84]

Davis completed *A Short History of the Confederate States of America* in October 1889. On November 6 he left Beauvoir to visit the plantation at Brierfield. On the steamboat trip upriver, he became ill; on the 13th he left Brierfield to return to New Orleans. Varina, who had taken another boat in order

Figure 10:
Postwar portrait of Jefferson Davis by Daniel Huntington

to reach Brierfield, met him on the river, and he finally received some medical care. They arrived in New Orleans on the 16th, and he was taken to the home of Charles Erasmus Fenner, an Associate Justice of the Louisiana Supreme Court. Though he remained in bed, he was stable for the next two weeks, but took a turn for the worse in early December. Just when he appeared to be improving, he lost consciousness on the evening of the 5th; he died at age 81 at 12:45 AM on Friday, December 6, 1889, in the presence of several friends and with his hand in Varina's.[85,86]

His funeral was one of the largest in the South, and included a continuous cortège, day and night, from New Orleans to Richmond.[87] Davis was first entombed at the Army of Northern Virginia tomb at Metairie Cemetery in New Orleans. In 1893, Mrs. Davis decided to transport his remains for burial at Hollywood Cemetery in Richmond.[88] After the remains were exhumed in New Orleans, they lay for a day at Memorial Hall of the newly organized Louisiana Historical Association, with many mourners passing by the casket, including Governor Murphy J. Foster, Sr. The body was then placed on a Louisville and Nashville Railroad car and transported to Richmond.[89]

Legacy

Many memorials to Jefferson Davis have been made throughout the United States. One notable example is the 351-foot (107 m) concrete obelisk located at the Jefferson Davis State Historic Site in Fairview, Kentucky, which marks the site of his birth (which was part of Christian County at that time). Construction on the monument began in 1917 and was finished in 1924.[90] Another example is the Jefferson Davis Presidential Library at Beauvoir in Biloxi, Mississippi. It was dedicated in 1998, suffered heavy damage during Hurricane Katrina in 2005, and reopened in 2008.[91]

Based at Rice University in Houston, Texas, *The Papers of Jefferson Davis* is an editing project that has been gathering and publishing documents related to Jefferson Davis since the early 1960s and has published 12 volumes, the first in 1971 and the most recent in 2008; 3 more volumes are planned. The project has roughly 100,000 documents in its archives.[92]

The birthday of Jefferson Davis is commemorated in several states. His actual birthday, June 3, is celebrated in Florida,[93] Kentucky,[94] Louisiana[95] and Tennessee;[96] in Alabama, it is celebrated on the first Monday in June.[97] In Mississippi, the last Monday of May (Memorial Day) is celebrated as "National Memorial Day and Jefferson Davis' Birthday".[98] In Texas, "Confederate Heroes Day" is celebrated on January 19, the birthday of Robert E. Lee;[96] Jefferson Davis' birthday had been officially celebrated on June 3 but was combined with Lee's birthday in 1973.[99]

In 1913, the United Daughters of the Confederacy conceived the Jefferson Davis Memorial Highway, a transcontinental highway that would travel through the South.[100] Portions of the highway's route in Virginia, Alabama and other states still bear the name of Jefferson Davis.[100] On September 20, 2011, the County Board of Arlington County, Virginia voted to change the name of "Old Jefferson Davis Highway" (the original route of the road in the County) after the chairman of the Board, who was originally from the Northeast, stated: "I have a problem with 'Jefferson Davis' ... There are aspects of our history I'm not particularly interested in celebrating".[101]

Bibliography

Secondary sources

- Allen, Felicity (1999). *Jefferson Davis: Unconquerable Heart*[102]. Columbia: The University of Missouri Press.
- Ballard, Michael B. (1986). *Long Shadow: Jefferson Davis and the Final Days of the Confederacy*[103]. Jackson: University Press of Mississippi.
- Collins, Donald E. (2005). *The Death and Resurrection of Jefferson Davis*. Lanham, MD: Rowman & Littlefield Publishers.
- Cooper, William J. (2000). *Jefferson Davis, American*. New York: Alfred A. Knopf.
- Cooper, William J. (2008). *Jefferson Davis and the Civil War Era*. Baton Rouge: Louisiana State University Press.
- Current, Richard, *et al.* (1993). *Encyclopedia of the Confederacy*. New York: Simon & Schuster.
- Davis, William C. (1991). *Jefferson Davis: The Man and His Hour*. New York: HarperCollins.
- Dodd, William E. (1907). *Jefferson Davis*[104]. Philadelphia: George W. Jacobs and Company.
- Eaton, Clement (1977). *Jefferson Davis*. New York: The Free Press.
- Escott, Paul (1978). *After Secession: Jefferson Davis and the Failure of Confederate Nationalism*. Baton Rouge: Louisiana State University Press.
- Hattaway, Herman and Beringer, Richard E. (2002). *Jefferson Davis, Confederate President*. Lawrence: University Press of Kansas.
- Neely Jr., Mark E. (1993). *Confederate Bastille: Jefferson Davis and Civil Liberties*[105]. Milwaukee: Marquette University Press.
- Patrick, Rembert W. (1944). *Jefferson Davis and His Cabinet*. Baton Rouge: Louisiana State University Press.
- Rable, George C. (1994). *The Confederate Republic: A Revolution against Politics*[106]. Chapel Hill: University of North Carolina Press.
- Stoker, Donald, "There Was No Offensive-Defensive Confederate Strategy," *Journal of Military History*, 73 (April 2009), 571-90.
- Strode, Hudson (1955). *Jefferson Davis, Volume I: American Patriot*. New York: Harcourt, Brace & Company.
- Strode, Hudson (1959). *Jefferson Davis, Volume II: Confederate President*. New York: Harcourt, Brace & Company.
- Strode, Hudson (1964). *Jefferson Davis, Volume III: Tragic Hero*. New York: Harcourt, Brace & Company.
- Swanson, James L. (2010). *Bloody Crimes: The Chase for Jefferson Davis and the Death Pageant for Lincoln's Corpse*. New York: HarperCollins.

- Thomas, Emory M. (1979). *The Confederate Nation, 1861–1865*. New York: Harper & Row.

Primary sources

- Davis, Jefferson (2003). Cooper, Jr., William J. ed. *Jefferson Davis: The Essential Writings*.
- Davis, Jefferson (1881). *The Rise and Fall of the Confederate Government*.
- Rowland, Dunbar, ed (1923). *Jefferson Davis, Constitutionalist: His Letters, Papers, and Speeches*. Jackson: Mississippi Department of Archives and History.
- Monroe, Jr., Haskell M.; McIntosh, James T.; Crist, Lynda L., eds (1971-2008). *The Papers of Jefferson Davis*. Louisiana State University Press.

External links

- Jefferson Davis in *Encyclopedia Virginia*[107]
- Jefferson Davis's final resting place[108]
- Works by Jefferson Davis[109] at Project Gutenberg
- Jefferson Davis[110] at the *Biographical Directory of the United States Congress*

President of the Provisional Confederate Congress

Howell Cobb

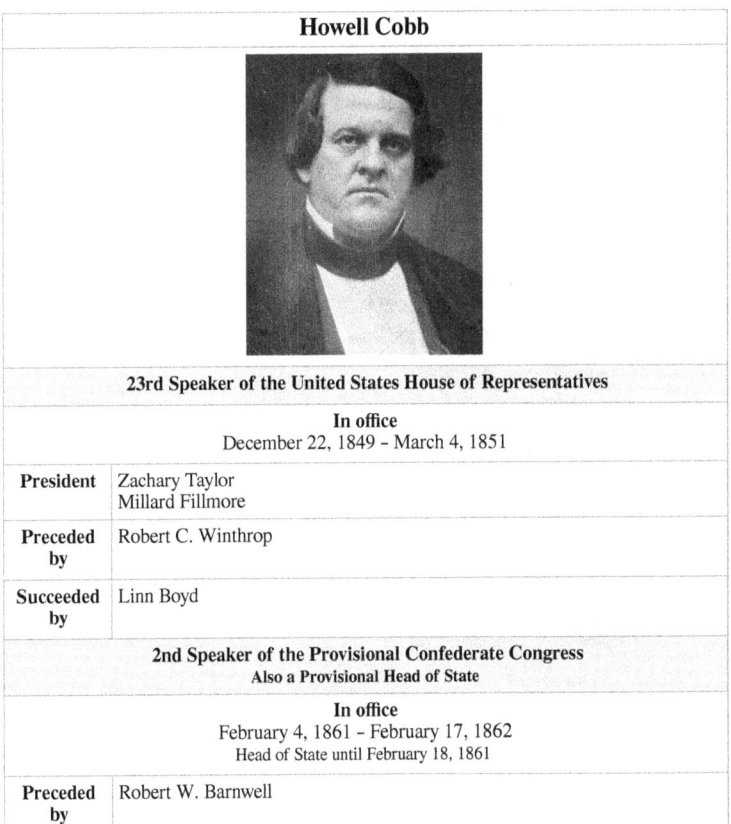

Howell Cobb	
23rd Speaker of the United States House of Representatives	
In office December 22, 1849 – March 4, 1851	
President	Zachary Taylor Millard Fillmore
Preceded by	Robert C. Winthrop
Succeeded by	Linn Boyd
2nd Speaker of the Provisional Confederate Congress Also a Provisional Head of State	
In office February 4, 1861 – February 17, 1862 Head of State until February 18, 1861	
Preceded by	Robert W. Barnwell

Succeeded by	Thomas Stanley Bocock (Speaker) Jefferson Davis (Head of State)
Member of U.S. House of Representatives from Georgia's At-large district	
In office March 4, 1843 – March 3, 1845	
Preceded by	Julius C. Alford, Edward J. Black, Walter T. Colquitt, Thomas F. Foster, Roger L. Gamble, George W. Crawford, Thomas B. King, James A. Meriwether, Mark A. Cooper, Lott Warren (General ticket)
Succeeded by	None; Representatives subsequently elected by district
Member of U.S. House of Representatives from Georgia's 6th district	
In office March 4, 1845 – March 4, 1851	
Preceded by	None; first elected
Succeeded by	Junius Hillyer
40th Governor of Georgia	
In office November 5, 1851 – November 9, 1853	
Preceded by	George W. Towns
Succeeded by	Herschel V. Johnson
22nd United States Secretary of the Treasury	
In office March 7, 1857 – December 8, 1860	
President	James Buchanan
Preceded by	James Guthrie
Succeeded by	Philip F. Thomas
Personal details	
Born	September 7, 1815 Jefferson County, Georgia
Died	October 9, 1868 (aged 53) New York City, New York
Political party	Democratic
Alma mater	University of Georgia
Profession	Law

Military service	
Service/branch	Confederate States Army
Rank	Major General
Unit	Army of Northern Virginia District of Georgia and Florida
Battles/wars	American Civil War

(Thomas) Howell Cobb (September 7, 1815 - October 9, 1868) was an American political figure. A Southern Democrat, Cobb was a five-term member of the United States House of Representatives and Speaker of the House from 1849 to 1851. He also served as a Secretary of Treasury under President James Buchanan (1857-1860) and the 40th Governor of Georgia (1851-1853).

He is, however, probably best known as one of the founders of the Confederate States of America, having served as the President of the Provisional Confederate Congress, when delegates of the secessionist states issued creation of the Confederacy.

Cobb served for two weeks between the foundation of the Confederacy and the election of Jefferson Davis as first President. This made him, as the Speaker of the Congress, provisional Head of State at this time.

Early life and career

Born in Jefferson County, Georgia, Cobb was raised in Athens, Georgia, and attended the University of Georgia where he was a member of the Phi Kappa Literary Society. He was admitted to the bar in 1836 and became solicitor general of the western judicial circuit of Georgia.

He married Mary Ann Lamar on May 26, 1835. They would have eleven children, the first in 1838 and the last in 1861. Several did not survive out of childhood, including their last, a son who was named after Howell's brother, Thomas Reade Rootes Cobb.

Congressman

He was elected as Democrat to the 28th, 29th, 30th and 31st Congresses. He was chairman of the U.S. House Committee on Mileage during the 28th Congress, and Speaker of the United States House of Representatives during the 31st Congress.

He sided with President Andrew Jackson on the question of nullification; was an efficient supporter of President James K. Polk's administration during the

Figure 11: *President Buchanan and his Cabinet*
From left to right: Jacob Thompson, Lewis Cass, John B. Floyd, James Buchanan, Howell Cobb, Isaac Toucey, Joseph Holt and Jeremiah S. Black, (c. 1859)

Mexican-American War; and was an ardent advocate of slavery extension into the territories, but when the Compromise of 1850 had been agreed upon, he became its staunch supporter as a Union Democrat. He joined Georgia Whigs Alexander Stephens and Robert Toombs in a statewide campaign to elect delegates to a state convention that overwhelmingly affirmed, in the Georgia Platform, that the state accepted the Compromise as the final resolution to the outstanding slavery issues. On that issue, Cobb was elected governor of Georgia by a large majority.

Speaker of the House

In 1850, as Speaker he would have been next in line to the Presidency for two days due to Vice Presidential vacancy and a president pro tempore not being appointed yet, except he did not meet the minimum eligibility for the presidency of being 35 years old. When Zachary Taylor died on July 9, Vice President Millard Fillmore became President. The president pro tempore of the Senate was not appointed until July 11 when William Rufus de Vane King took that position.

Governor of Georgia

In 1851, he left the House to serve as the Governor of Georgia, holding that post until 1853. He published *A Scriptural Examination of the Institution of Slavery* (1856).[111]

Return to Congress and Secretary of the Treasury

He was elected to the 34th Congress and then took the position of Secretary of the Treasury in Buchanan's Cabinet. He served for three years, resigning in December 1860. At one time, Cobb was Buchanan's choice for his successor.[112]

A Founder of the Confederacy

In 1860, Cobb ceased to be a Unionist, and became a leader of the secession movement. He was president of a convention of the seceded states that assembled in Montgomery, Alabama, on February 24, 1861. Under Cobb's guidance, the delegates drafted a constitution for the new Confederacy. He served as President of several sessions of the Confederate Provisional Congress, before resigning to join the military when war erupted.

Civil War

Cobb enlisted in the Confederate Army and was named as colonel of the 16th Georgia Infantry. He was appointed a brigadier general on February 13, 1862, and assigned command of a brigade in what became the Army of Northern Virginia. Between February and June 1862, he represented the Confederate authorities in negotiations with Union officers for an agreement on the exchange of prisoners of war. His efforts in these discussions contributed to the Dix-Hill Cartel accord reached in July 1862.[113]

Cobb saw combat during the Peninsula Campaign and the Seven Days Battles. Cobb's brigade played a key role in the fighting at Crampton's Gap during the Battle of South Mountain, where it arrived at a critical time to delay a Union advance through the gap. His men also fought at the subsequent Battle of Antietam.

In October 1862, Cobb was detached from the Army of Northern Virginia and sent to the District of Middle Florida. He was promoted to major general on September 9, 1863, and placed in command of the District of Georgia and Florida. He suggested the construction of a prisoner-of-war camp in southern Georgia, a location thought to be safe from Union invaders. This idea led to the creation of Andersonville prison. When William T. Sherman's armies entered Georgia during the 1864 Atlanta Campaign and subsequent March to

Figure 12: *Howell Cobb in his postbellum days*

the Sea, General Cobb commanded the Georgia reserve corps. In the spring of 1865, with the Confederacy clearly waning, he and his troops were sent to Columbus, Georgia to help oppose Wilson's Raid. He led the hopeless Confederate resistance in the Battle of Columbus, Georgia on Easter Sunday, April 16, 1865.

During Sherman's March to the Sea, the army camped one night near Cobb's plantation. When Sherman discovered that the house he planned to stay in for the night belonged to Cobb, whom Sherman described in his *Memoirs* as "one of the leading rebels of the South, then a general in the Southern army," he confiscated Cobb's property and leveled the plantation, instructing his subordinates to "spare nothing."[114]

In the closing days of the war, Cobb fruitlessly opposed General Robert E. Lee's eleventh hour proposal of enlisting slaves into the army. Fearing this move would completely discredit the fundamental justification of slavery that blacks were inferior people, he said, "You cannot make soldiers of slaves, or slaves of soldiers. The day you make a soldier of them is the beginning of the end of the Revolution. And if slaves seem good soldiers, then our whole theory of slavery is wrong."[115]

He surrendered at Macon, Georgia, April 20, 1865.

Postbellum

Following the war, Cobb returned home and resumed his law practice, but despite pressure from his former constituents and soldiers, he refused to make any public remarks on Reconstruction policy until he received a presidential pardon, although he privately opposed it. Finally receiving that document in early 1868, he then vigorously opposed the Reconstruction Acts, making a series of speeches that summer that bitterly denounced the policies of the reigning Radical Republicans in Congress.

Taking a break from his schedule of political speeches, Cobb decided to vacation in New York City in the autumn. He died of a heart attack there. His body was returned to Athens, Georgia, for burial in Oconee Hill Cemetery.[116]

Thomas Willis Cobb was a cousin and Thomas Reade Rootes Cobb a younger brother of Howell Cobb. His great uncle and namesake, Howell Cobb, had been a U.S. Congressman from 1807-1812, and then served as an officer in the War of 1812.

References

- This article incorporates text from a publication now in the public domain: Chisholm, Hugh, ed (1911). *Encyclopædia Britannica* (11th ed.). Cambridge University Press.
- Ⓟ *This article incorporates public domain material from websites or documents*[117] *of the Biographical Directory of the United States Congress.*
- Howell Cobb[118] at the *Biographical Directory of the United States Congress* Retrieved on 2009-04-17
- US Department of War (1880 - 1901). The War of the Rebellion: A Compilation of the Official Records of the Union and Confederate Armies. Washington: Government Printing Office.

Further reading

- Montgomery, Horace, *Howell Cobb's Confederate Career.* (Tuscaloosa, Alabama: Confederate Publishing, 1959).

External links

- New Georgia Encyclopedia: Howell Cobb (1815-1868)[119]
- U.S. Treasury - Biography of Secretary Howell Cobb[120]
- "Howell Cobb"[121]. Find a Grave. Retrieved 2008-02-13.
- "The Late Howell Cobb"[122], Southern Recorder, November 10, 1868. Atlanta Historic Newspaper Archive. Digital Library of Georgia

Vice President

Alexander H. Stephens

This is an article about the Confederate Vice President. For the shipbuilding company, see Alexander Stephen and Sons

Alexander Stephens	

Vice President of the Confederate States of America	
In office February 11, 1861 – May 11, 1865	
President	Jefferson Davis
Preceded by	*Office instituted*
Succeeded by	*Office abolished*
50th Governor of Georgia	
In office November 4, 1882 – March 4, 1883	
Preceded by	Alfred H. Colquitt
Succeeded by	James S. Boynton

\multicolumn{2}{c}{**Member of the U.S. House of Representatives from Georgia's 8th district**}
\multicolumn{2}{c}{**In office** December 1, 1873 – November 4, 1882}
Preceded by	John James Jones
Succeeded by	Seaborn Reese
\multicolumn{2}{c}{**In office** October 2, 1843 – March 3, 1859}
Preceded by	Mark Anthony Cooper
Succeeded by	John James Jones
\multicolumn{2}{c}{**Personal details**}
Born	February 11, 1812 Taliaferro County, Georgia
Died	March 4, 1883 (aged 71) Atlanta, Georgia
Nationality	American
Political party	Whig, Constitutional, Democratic
Profession	Lawyer
Religion	Presbyterian
Signature	*Alexander H. Stephens*

Alexander Hamilton Stephens (February 11, 1812 – March 4, 1883) was an American politician from Georgia. He was Vice President of the Confederate States of America during the American Civil War. He also served as a U.S. Representative from Georgia (both before the Civil War and after Reconstruction) and as the 50th Governor of Georgia from 1882 until his death in 1883.

Early life and career

Stephens was born to Andrew B. and Margaret Grier Stephens on a farm near Crawfordville, Taliaferro County, Georgia. (At the time of his birth, the farm was part of Warren County and Crawfordville had not yet been founded.) He grew up poor and in difficult circumstances. His mother died when he was an infant and his father and stepmother, Matilda Stephens, died days apart when he was 14, causing him and several siblings to be scattered among relatives.

Frail but precocious, the young Stephens acquired his continued education through the generosity of several benefactors. One of them was the Presbyterian minister Alexander Hamilton Webster. Out of respect for his mentor,

Stephens adopted Webster's middle name, Hamilton, as his own. Stephens attended the Franklin College (later the University of Georgia) in Athens, where he was roommates with Crawford W. Long and a member of the Phi Kappa Literary Society. He graduated at the top of his class in 1832.

After several unhappy years teaching school, he took up legal studies, passed the bar in 1834, and began a successful career as a lawyer in Crawfordville. During his 32 years of practice, he gained a reputation as a capable defender of the wrongfully accused. None of his clients charged with capital crimes were executed. One notable case was that of a slave woman accused of attempted murder. Stephens volunteered to defend her. Despite the circumstantial evidence presented against her, Stephens persuaded the jury to acquit the woman, thus saving her life.

Stephens was extremely sickly throughout his life. He often weighed less than 100 pounds,[123] sometimes considerably less, and was frequently bedridden and near death. Descriptions of his unhealthy appearance were common in newspaper stories. While his voice was described as shrill and unpleasant, at the beginning of the Civil War a Northern newspaper described him as "the Strongest Man in the South" because of his intelligence, judgment, and eloquence. His generosity was legendary; his house, even when he was governor of Georgia, was always open to travelers or tramps, and he personally financed the education of over 100 students, black and white, male and female. So prodigious was his charity, that he died virtually penniless.

As his wealth increased, Stephens began acquiring land and slaves. By the time of the Civil War, Stephens owned 34 slaves and several thousand acres. Stephens entered politics in 1836, when he was elected to the Georgia House of Representatives. He served there until 1841. In 1842, he was elected to the Georgia State Senate.

Congressional career

In 1843, Stephens was elected U.S. Representative as a Whig, in a special election to fill the vacancy caused by the resignation of Mark A. Cooper. This seat was at-large, as Georgia did not have House districts until 1844. In 1844, 1846, and 1848, Stephens was re-elected from the 7th District as a Whig. In 1851 he was re-elected as a Unionist, in 1853 as a Whig (from the 8th District), and in 1855 and 1857 as a Democrat. He served from October 2, 1843 to March 3, 1859, from the 28th Congress through the 35th Congress.

As a national lawmaker during the crucial decades before the Civil War, Stephens was involved in all of the major sectional battles. He began as a moderate defender of slavery, but later accepted the prevailing Southern rationale used to defend the institution.

Stephens quickly rose to prominence as one of the leading Southern Whigs in the House. He supported the annexation of Texas in 1845. Along with his fellow Whigs, he vehemently opposed the Mexican-American War. He was an equally vigorous opponent of the Wilmot Proviso, which would have barred the extension of slavery into territories acquired by the United States during the war with Mexico. This would later nearly kill Stephens when he argued with Judge Francis H. Cone, who stabbed him repeatedly in a fit of anger.[124] Stephens was physically outmatched by his larger assailant, but he remained defiant during the attack, refusing to recant his positions even at the cost of his life. Only the intervention of others saved him. Stephens' wounds were serious, and he returned home to Crawfordville to recover. He and Cone reconciled before Cone's death in 1859.

Stephens and fellow Georgia Representative Robert Toombs campaigned for the election of Zachary Taylor as President in 1848. Both were chagrined and angered when Taylor proved less than pliable on aspects of the Compromise of 1850. Stephens and Toombs both supported the Compromise of 1850 though they opposed the exclusion of slavery from the territories on the theory that such lands belonged to all of the people. The pair returned to Georgia to secure support for the measures at home. Both men were instrumental in the drafting and approval of the Georgia Platform, which rallied Unionists throughout the Deep South.

Not only were Stephens and Toombs political allies, but they were lifelong friends. Stephens was described as "a highly sensitive young man of serious and joyless habits of consuming ambition, of poverty-fed pride, and of morbid preoccupation within self," a contrast to the "robust, wealthy, and convivial Toombs. But this strange camaraderie endured with singular accord throughout their lives."[125]

By this time, Stephens had departed the ranks of the Whig party — its northern wing having proved obstinate to Southern interests. Back in Georgia, Stephens, Toombs, and Democratic Representative Howell Cobb formed the Constitutional Union Party. The party overwhelmingly carried the state in the ensuing election and, for the first time, Stephens returned to Congress no longer a Whig. Stephens spent the next few years as a Constitutional Unionist, essentially an independent. He vigorously opposed the dismantling of the Constitutional Union Party when it began crumbling in 1851. Political realities soon forced the Union Democrats in the party to affiliate once more with the national party, and by mid-1852, the combination of both Democrats and Whigs, which had formed a "party" behind the Compromise, had ended.

The sectional issue surged to the forefront again in 1854, when Senator Stephen A. Douglas moved to organize the Nebraska Territory, all of which lay north of the Missouri Compromise line, in the Kansas-Nebraska Act. This legislation

Figure 13: *Alexander Stephens*

aroused fury in the North because it applied the popular sovereignty principle to the Territory, thereby negating the Missouri Compromise. Had it not been for Stephens, the bill would have probably never passed in the House. He employed an obscure House rule to bring the bill to a vote. He later called this "the greatest glory of my life."

From this point on, Stephens voted with the Democrats. Not until after the Congressional elections of 1855 could Stephens be properly called a Democrat, although even then he never officially declared it. In this move, Stephens broke irrevocably with many of his former Whig colleagues. When the Whig Party disintegrated after the election of 1852, some Whigs flocked to the short-lived Know-Nothing Party. But Stephens fiercely opposed the Know-Nothings both for their secrecy and their anti-immigrant and anti-Catholic position.

Despite his late arrival in the Democratic Party, Stephens quickly rose through the ranks. He even served as President James Buchanan's floor manager in the House during the fruitless battle for the Lecompton Constitution for Kansas Territory in 1857. He was instrumental in framing and passing the so-called English bill after it became clear that Lecompton would never pass.

Stephens did not seek re-election to Congress in 1858. As sectional peace eroded during the next two years, Stephens became increasingly critical of southern extremists. Although virtually the entire South had spurned Douglas

Figure 14: *The original Confederate Cabinet. L-R: Judah P. Benjamin, Stephen Mallory, Christopher Memminger, Alexander Stephens, LeRoy Pope Walker, Jefferson Davis, John H. Reagan and Robert Toombs.*

as a traitor to Southern Rights because he had opposed the Lecompton Constitution and broken with Buchanan, Stephens remained on good terms with the Illinois Senator and served as one of his presidential electors in the election of 1860.

Vice President of the Confederacy

In 1861, Stephens was elected as a delegate to the Georgia special convention to decide on secession from the United States. During the convention, as well as during the 1860 presidential campaign, Stephens called for the South to remain loyal to the Union, likening it to a leaking but fixable boat. During the convention he reminded his fellow delegates that Republicans were a minority in Congress (especially in the Senate) and, even with a Republican President, would be forced to compromise just as the two sections had for decades. And, because the Supreme Court had voted 7-2 in the Dred Scott case, it would take decades of Senate-approved appointments to reverse it. He voted against secession in the convention, but asserted the right to secede if the federal government continued allowing northern states to nullify the Fugitive Slave Law with "personal liberty laws". He was elected to the Confederate Congress, and was chosen by the Congress as Vice President of the provisional government. He was then elected Vice President of the Confederacy. He took the

Figure 15: *Stephens in his later years*

oath of office on February 11, 1861, and served until his arrest on May 11, 1865. Stephens officially served in office eight days longer than President Jefferson Davis; he took his oath seven days before Davis' inauguration and was captured the day after Davis.

On March 21, 1861, Stephens gave his famous Cornerstone Speech in Savannah, Georgia. In it he declared that slavery was the natural condition of blacks and the foundation of the Confederacy. He declared that, "Our new Government is founded upon exactly the opposite ideas; its foundations are laid, its cornerstone rests, upon the great truth that the negro is not equal to the white man; that slavery, subordination to the superior race, is his natural and normal condition."[126]

On the eve of the outbreak of the Civil War, he counseled delay in moving militarily against the Northern-held Fort Sumter and Fort Pickens, so that the Confederacy could build up its forces and stock resources.[127]

In 1862, Stephens first publicly expressed his opposition to the Davis Administration.[128] Throughout the war he denounced many of the president's policies, including conscription, suspension of the writ of *habeas corpus*, impressment, various financial and taxation policies, and Davis' military strategy.

In mid-1863, Davis dispatched Stephens on a fruitless mission to Washington to discuss prisoner exchanges, but in the immediate aftermath of the Federal

Figure 16: *John White Alexander's portrait of Alexander Stephens*

victory of Gettysburg, the Lincoln Administration refused to receive him. As the war continued, and the fortunes of the Confederacy sank lower, Stephens became more outspoken in his opposition to the administration. On March 16, 1864, Stephens delivered a speech to the Georgia Legislature that was widely reported both North and South. In it, he excoriated the Davis Administration for its support of conscription and suspension of *habeas corpus*, and further, he supported a block of resolutions aimed at securing peace. From then until the end of the war, as he continued to press for actions aimed at bringing about peace, his relations with Davis, never warm to begin with, turned completely sour.

On February 3, 1865, he was one of three Confederate commissioners who met with Lincoln on the steamer *River Queen* at the Hampton Roads Conference, a fruitless effort to discuss measures to bring an end to the fight.

Post-bellum career

Stephens was arrested at his home in Crawfordville, on May 11, 1865. He was imprisoned in Fort Warren, Boston Harbor, for five months until October 1865. In 1866, he was elected to the United States Senate by the first legislature convened under the new Georgia State Constitution, but did not present his credentials, as the state had not been readmitted to the union. In 1873, he

Figure 17: *Alexander Stephens gravesite memorial at Liberty Hall*

was elected U.S. Representative as a Democrat from the 8th District to fill the vacancy caused by the death of Ambrose R. Wright, and was re-elected in 1874, 1876, 1878, and 1880. He served in the 43rd through 47th Congresses, from December 1, 1873 until his resignation on November 4, 1882. On that date, he was elected and took office as Governor of Georgia. His tenure as governor proved brief; Stephens died on March 4, 1883, four months after taking office. According to a former slave, a gate fell on Stephens "and he was crippled and lamed up from dat time on 'til he died."[129]

He was interred in Oakland Cemetery in Atlanta, then re-interred on his estate, Liberty Hall, near Crawfordville.

He is the author of *A Constitutional View of the Late War Between the States* (1867-70, 2 Vols.) and *History of the United States* (1871 and 1883).

He is pictured on the CSA $20.00 banknote (3rd, 5th, 6th, and 7th issues).

Stephens County, Georgia, bears his name, as does A. H. Stephens Historic Park, a state park near Crawfordville.

References

- Rudolph R. von Abele, *Alexander H. Stephens: A Biography* (1946)

- Henry Cleveland, *Alexander H. Stephens in Public and Private, with Letters and Speeches*[130] (1866)
- William C. Davis, *The Union that Shaped the Confederacy: Robert Toombs & Alexander H. Stephens* (2002)
- Richard Malcolm Johnston & William Hand Browne, *Life of Alexander H. Stephens*[131] (1878).
- Louis Pendleton, *Alexander H. Stephens*[132] (1908)
- Thomas E. Schott, *Alexander H. Stephens of Georgia: A Biography* (1988)
- W. P. Trent, *Southern Statesmen of the Old Régime*[133] (1897)
- Jon L. Wakelyn, *Biographical Dictionary of the Confederacy*
- Wilson, Edmund. *Patriotic Gore: Studies in the Literature of the American Civil War* (1962) ch 11, on his book
- Biographical article from *Harper's Weekly*, February 23, 1861.

External links

- Alexander H. Stephens[134] at the *Biographical Directory of the United States Congress* Retrieved on 2009-03-22
- Timeline and biography of Alexander Stephens[135]
- The Alexander H. Stephens papers[136], containing correspondence while Stephens was vice president of the Confederacy, are available for research use at the Historical Society of Pennsylvania.
- The Life and Work of Alexander Stephens[137]
- "Cornerstone" Speech[138]
- What I Really Said in the Cornerstone Speech[139] Stephens clarifies his statements
- Another explanation[140]
- A. H. Stephens State Historic Park[141]

Secretary of State: Toombs, Hunter, Benjamin*

Robert Toombs

Robert Augustus Toombs	
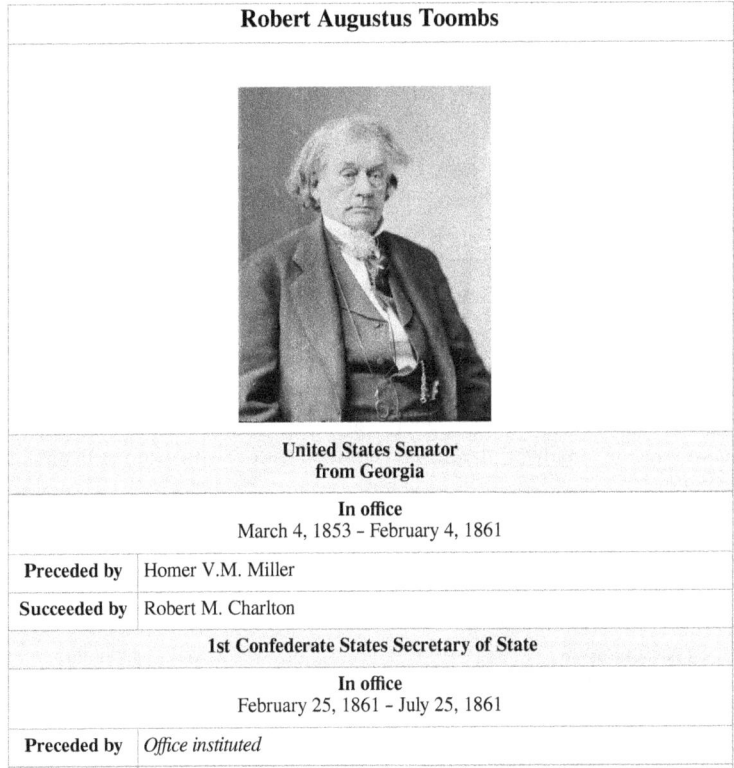	
United States Senator from Georgia	
In office March 4, 1853 - February 4, 1861	
Preceded by	Homer V.M. Miller
Succeeded by	Robert M. Charlton
1st Confederate States Secretary of State	
In office February 25, 1861 - July 25, 1861	
Preceded by	*Office instituted*
Succeeded by	Robert M. T. Hunter

	Personal details
Born	July 2, 1810 Wilkes County, Georgia, U.S.
Died	December 15, 1885 (aged 75) Washington, Georgia, U.S.
Political party	Whig, Democrat
Spouse(s)	Julia A. Dubose
Alma mater	Franklin College of Arts and Sciences (University of Georgia) Union College University of Virginia Law School
Profession	Politician, Lawyer
Religion	Methodist

Robert Augustus Toombs (July 2, 1810 - December 15, 1885) was an American political leader, United States Senator from Georgia, 1st Secretary of State of the Confederacy, and a Confederate general in the Civil War.

Early life

Born near Washington, Wilkes County, Georgia, Robert Augustus Toombs was the fifth child of Catherine Huling and Robert Toombs. His father died when he was five, and he entered Franklin College at the University of Georgia in Athens when he was just fourteen. During his time at Franklin College he was a member of the Demosthenian Literary Society, which honors him as one of its most legendary alumni to this day. After the university chastised him for unbecoming conduct in a card-playing incident, Toombs continued his education at Union College, in Schenectady, New York, from which he graduated in 1828. Toombs went on to study law at the University of Virginia Law School in Charlottesville. Shortly after his admission to the Georgia bar, he married his childhood sweetheart, Julia A. Dubose, with whom he had three children.

Public service

Toombs was admitted to the bar in 1830, and served in the Georgia House of Representatives (1838, 1840-1841, and 1843-1844). His genial character, proclivity for entertainment, and unqualified success on the legal circuit earned Toombs the growing attention and admiration of his fellow Georgians. On the wave of his growing popularity, Toombs won a seat to the United States House

Figure 18: *Robert Toombs*

of Representatives (1844-1853), and joined his close friend and fellow representative Alexander H. Stephens from Crawfordville, Georgia. Their friendship forged a powerful personal and political bond that effectively defined and articulated Georgia's position on national issues in the middle decades of the nineteenth century. Toombs, like Stephens, emerged as a states' rights partisan, became a national Whig, and once the Whig Party dissolved, aided in the creation of the short-lived Constitutional Union Party in the early 1850s.

Toombs stood with most Whigs regarding the status of Texas as the 28th state. Historian William Y. Thompson writes that Toombs was "prepared to vote all necessary supplies to repel invasion. But he did not agree that the territory between the Nueces and the Rio Grande rivers was a part of Texas. He declared the movement of American forces to the Rio Grande at President Polk's command 'was contrary to the laws of this country, a usurpation on the rights of this House, and an aggression on the rights of Mexico."[142]

From 1853 to 1861 Toombs served in the United States Senate, only reluctantly joining the Democratic Party when lack of interest among other states doomed the Constitutional Union Party.

From Unionist to Confederate

Throughout the 1840s and 1850s, Toombs fought to reconcile national policies with sectional interests. He had opposed the Annexation of Texas but vowed to defend the new state once it was annexed late in 1845. He also opposed the Mexican-American War, President Polk's Oregon policy, the Walker Tariff of 1846 and the Wilmot Proviso, first introduced in 1846. In common with Alexander H. Stephens and Howell Cobb, he defended Henry Clay's Compromise of 1850 against southerners who advocated secession from the Union as the only solution to sectional tensions over slavery. He denounced the Nashville Convention, opposed the secessionists in Georgia, and helped to frame the famous Georgia platform (1850). His position and that of Southern Unionists during the decade 1850-1860 has often been misunderstood. They disapproved of secession, not because they considered it wrong in principle, but because they considered it inexpedient.

Toombs objected to halting the spread of slavery into the territories of California and New Mexico and even the abolishment of what John C. Calhoun had called the "peculiar institution" in Washington, D.C. He took the view that the territories were the common property of all the people of the United States and that Congress must insure equal treatment to both slaveholder and non-slaveholder. Were the rights of the South violated, Toombs declared, "Let discord reign forever."[143]

Toombs favored the Kansas-Nebraska Act, the admission of Kansas under the Lecompton Constitution, and the English Bill (1858). However, his faith in the resiliency and effectiveness of the national government to resolve sectional conflicts waned as the 1850s drew to a close.

On June 24, 1856, Toombs introduced in the Senate the Toombs Bill, which proposed a constitutional convention in Kansas under conditions which were acknowledged by various anti-slavery leaders as fair, and which mark the greatest concessions made by the pro-slavery senators during the Kansas struggle. The bill did not provide for the submission of the constitution to popular vote, and the silence on this point of the territorial law under which the Lecompton Constitution of Kansas was framed in 1857 was the crux of the Lecompton struggle.

Thompson refers to Toombs as "hardly a man of the people with his wealth and imperious manner. But his handsome imposing appearance, undoubted ability, and boldness of speech appealed to Georgians, who kept him in national office until the Civil War brought him home."[144]

Figure 19: *The original Confederate Cabinet. L-R: Judah P. Benjamin, Stephen Mallory, Christopher Memminger, Alexander Stephens, LeRoy Pope Walker, Jefferson Davis, John H. Reagan and Robert Toombs.*

Secession and Civil War

In the presidential campaign of 1860 he supported John C. Breckinridge, and on December 22, soon after the election of Abraham Lincoln, sent a telegram to Georgia that asserted that "secession by the 4th of March next should be thundered forth from the ballot-box by the united voice of Georgia." He delivered a farewell address in the Senate (January 7, 1861) in which he said: "We want no negro equality, no negro citizenship; we want no negro race to degrade our own; and as one man [we] would meet you upon the border with the sword in one hand and the torch in the other."[145] He returned to Georgia, and with Governor Joseph E. Brown led the fight for secession against Stephens and Herschel V. Johnson (1812-1880). His influence was a most powerful factor in inducing the "old-line Whigs" to support immediate secession.

Unlike the crises of 1850, these events galvanized Toombs and energized ambitions for becoming the president of the new Confederate nation. The selection of Jefferson Davis as the new nation's chief executive not only dashed Toombs's highest hopes but also turned him into one of the most outspoken critics of the Confederate government and its policies. Nevertheless, Davis chose Toombs as his first Confederate States Secretary of State. Toombs was the only member of the Davis administration to voice reservations about the attack on Fort Sumter. After reading Lincoln's letter to the governor of South

Figure 20: *Toombs' house in Washington, Georgia, 1934.*

Carolina, Toombs said memorably: "Mr. President, at this time it is suicide, murder, and will lose us every friend at the North. You will wantonly strike a hornet's nest which extends from mountain to ocean, and legions now quiet will swarm out and sting us to death. It is unnecessary; it puts us in the wrong; it is fatal." Within months of his appointment, a frustrated Toombs stepped down to join the Confederate States Army. He received a commission as a brigadier general on July 19, 1861, and served first as a brigade commander in the (Confederate) Army of the Potomac, and then in David R. Jones's division of the Army of Northern Virginia through the Peninsula Campaign, Seven Days Battles, Northern Virginia Campaign, and Maryland Campaign. He was wounded in the hand at the Battle of Antietam. He resigned his CSA commission on March 3, 1863, to become Colonel of the 3rd Cavalry of the Georgia Militia, and subsequently served as a brigadier general and adjutant and inspector-general of General Gustavus W. Smith's division of Georgia militia. Denied a military promotion, he resigned his commission and returned home to Washington, Georgia.

Final years

When the Confederacy finally collapsed in 1865, Toombs barely escaped arrest by Union troops and went into hiding until he fled to Cuba on November 4, and then to London and Paris. He returned to the United States via Canada in 1867. Because he refused to request a pardon from Congress, he never regained his American citizenship. He did restore his lucrative law practice as an "unreconstructed" southerner. In addition, he dominated the Georgia constitutional convention of 1877, where once again he demonstrated the political skill and temperament that earlier had earned him a reputation as one of Georgia's most effective leaders.

Legacy

Georgia's Toombs County is named for Robert Toombs. So is the Georgia town of Toomsboro, though with a slightly altered spelling. His legacy also lives on in his hometown of Washington, Georgia[146]. Visitors to Washington can tour the Robert Toombs House, a State Historic Site operated by the Georgia Department of Natural Resources.

Robert Toombs Christian Academy in Lyons, Georgia was named in his honor.

External links

- *Robert Toombs*[147], New Georgia Encyclopedia
- Eicher, John H., & Eicher, David J., *Civil War High Commands*, Stanford University Press, 2001, ISBN 0-8047-3641-3.
- Davis, William C., *The Union That Shaped the Confederacy: Robert Toombs and Alexander H. Stephens*. University Press of Kansas, 2001. Pp. xi, 284.
- Robert Toombs[148] at the *Biographical Directory of the United States Congress* Retrieved on 2008-02-13
- *The Life of Robert Toombs*[149]
- *Robert Toombs : Statesman, Speaker, Soldier, Sage*[150] at Project Gutenberg (Transcription of 1892 text)
- Robert Toombs' Letters to Julia Ann Dubose Toombs, 1850-1867[151], Digital Library of Georgia

Robert M. T. Hunter

Robert Mercer Taliaferro Hunter	

18th Speaker of the United States House of Representatives	
In office December 16, 1839 – March 4, 1841	
President	Martin Van Buren
Preceded by	James K. Polk
Succeeded by	John White
Member of the U.S. House of Representatives from Virginia's 9th district	
In office March 4, 1837 – March 4, 1843	
Preceded by	John Roane
Succeeded by	Samuel Chilton
Member of the U.S. House of Representatives from Virginia's 8th district	
In office March 4, 1845 – March 4, 1847	
Preceded by	Willoughby Newton
Succeeded by	Richard L. T. Beale
United States Senator from Virginia	
In office March 4, 1847 – March 28, 1861	
Preceded by	William S. Archer
Succeeded by	John S. Carlile
2nd Confederate States Secretary of State	
In office July 25, 1861 – February 22, 1862	
President	Jefferson Davis

Preceded by	Robert Toombs
Succeeded by	Judah P. Benjamin
Confederate States Senator from Virginia	
In office February 18, 1862 – May 10, 1865	
Preceded by	None
Succeeded by	None
Personal details	
Born	April 21, 1809 Essex County, Virginia
Died	July 18, 1887 (aged 78) Essex County, Virginia
Political party	Whig Democratic
Alma mater	University of Virginia
Profession	Law

Robert Mercer Taliaferro Hunter (April 21, 1809 – July 18, 1887) was an American statesman born in Essex County, Virginia.

Career

He entered the University of Virginia in his seventeenth year and was one of its first graduates. While he was a student, he became a member of the Jefferson Literary and Debating Society. He then studied law at the Winchester (Va.) Law School, and in 1830 was admitted to the bar. From 1835 to 1837 he was a member of the Virginia House of Delegates.

From 1837 to 1843, and again from 1845 to 1847, he was a member of the U.S. House of Representatives. He served as Speaker of the House from 1839 to 1841, and is the youngest person to have ever held that position. From 1847 to 1861 he was in the Senate, where he was chairman of the Committee on Finance (1850-1861). He is credited with having brought about a reduction of the quantity of silver in the smaller coins. He was the author of the Tariff of 1857 and of the bonded-warehouse system, and was one of the first to advocate civil service reform. In 1853 he declined President Millard Fillmore's offer to make him Secretary of State.

At the National Democratic Convention at Charleston, South Carolina in 1860, he was the Virginia delegation's choice as candidate for the presidency of the United States, but was defeated for the nomination by Stephen A. Douglas. Hunter did not regard Lincoln's election as being of itself a sufficient cause for

Figure 21: *Robert Mercer Taliaferro Hunter*

secession, and on January 11, 1861 he proposed an elaborate but impracticable scheme for the adjustment of differences between the North and the South, but when this and several other efforts to the same end had failed he quietly urged his own state to pass the ordinance of secession. He was expelled from the Senate for supporting secession.

From 1861 to 1862 he was the Confederate States Secretary of State; and from 1862 to 1865 was a member of the Confederate Senate, in which he was, at times, a caustic critic of the Davis administration. He was one of the commissioners to treat at the Hampton Roads Conference in 1865, and after the surrender of General Lee was summoned by President Lincoln to Richmond to confer regarding the restoration of Virginia in the Union. From 1874 to 1880 he was the treasurer of Virginia, and from 1885 until his death near Lloyds, Virginia, was collector of the Port of Tappahannock, Virginia.

Legacy

Among his works was *Origin of the Late War*, about the causes of the Civil War.

In 1942, a United States Liberty ship named the SS *Robert M. T. Hunter* was launched. She was scrapped in 1971.[152]

Hunter was pictured on the Confederate $10 bill.[153]

Figure 22: *Hunter in later life*

Further reading

Hunter, Martha T. (1903). *A Memoir of Robert M. T. Hunter*. Washington, DC: The Neale Publishing Company.

Anderson, Dice Robins (1906), "Robert Mercer Taliaferro Hunter", *The John P. Branch historical papers of Randolph-Macon College*, **vol. 2 no. 2**, pp. [4]-77

References

- Patrick, Rembert W. (1944). *Jefferson Davis and His Cabinet*. Baton Rouge: Louisiana State University Press. pp. 90-101.

External links

- Retrocession of Alexandria[154] - A speech by R. M. T. Hunter before the U.S. House of Representatives, May 8th, 1846
- Robert M. T. Hunter[155] at the *Biographical Directory of the United States Congress*. Retrieved April 29, 2009
- "Robert M. T. Hunter"[156]. Find a Grave. Retrieved April 29, 2009.

☺ *This article incorporates public domain material from websites or documents*[157] *of the Biographical Directory of the United States Congress.*

This article incorporates text from a publication now in the public domain: Chisholm, Hugh, ed (1911). *Encyclopædia Britannica* (11th ed.). Cambridge University Press.

Secretary of War : Walker, Benjamin*, Randolph, Seddon, Breckinridge

LeRoy Pope Walker

LeRoy Pope Walker	
1st Confederate States Secretary of War	
In office February 25, 1861 – September 16, 1861	
President	Jefferson Davis
Preceded by	*Office instituted*
Succeeded by	Judah P. Benjamin
Personal details	
Born	February 7, 1817 Huntsville, Alabama, U.S.

Died	August 23, 1884 (aged 67) U.S.
Political party	Democratic
Spouse(s)	Eliza Dickson Pickett
Profession	Politician
Religion	Presbyterian

LeRoy Pope Walker (February 7, 1817 – August 23, 1884) was the first Confederate States Secretary of War.

Early life and career

Walker was born near Huntsville, Alabama in 1817, the son of John Williams Walker and Matilda Pope, and a grandson of LeRoy Pope. He was educated by private tutors, then attended universities in Alabama and Virginia. Before reaching the age of 21, he was admitted to the bar. He held various offices in Alabama; in 1853, he resigned his position as a circuit court judge in order to focus on his legal practice. He actively promoted secession.[158] He married Eliza Dickson Pickett on July 29, 1850.

Civil War

Largely on the advice of several of Walker's supporters, including his brother Richard, President Davis appointed him to the post of Secretary of War, though Walker was not personally known to Davis. He was energetic and confident in support of the Confedracy, but had no military training. The stress and difficulties of his cabinet position seriously affected his health.[159] In March 1861, the Southern states that had seceded from the Union appointed special commissioners to travel to those other Southern states that had yet to secede. Walker was chosen as the Commissioner from Alabama to the Tennessee Secession Convention, where he publicly read Alabama's Articles of Secession and tried to persuade Tennessee politicians to vote to do likewise.

Starting in August 1861, Davis encouraged Walker to become a Confederate representative to Europe; Walker did not accept this, but on September 16 he resigned his post. Davis made him a brigadier general in the Confederate States Army, commanding army garrisons in Alabama, before resigning in March 1862.[160]

Figure 23: *The original Confederate Cabinet. L-R: Judah P. Benjamin, Stephen Mallory, Christopher Memminger, Alexander Stephens, LeRoy Pope Walker, Jefferson Davis, John H. Reagan and Robert Toombs*

Post-war

After the war, Walker returned to his legal practice and continued to be interested in politics. He died in 1887 and was buried in Maple Hill Cemetery in Huntsville.[161]

References

- "Leroy Pope Walker"[162]. The Confederate War Department. Retrieved 2011-08-13.

Bibliography

- Patrick, Rembert W. (1944). *Jefferson Davis and His Cabinet*. Baton Rouge: Louisiana State University Press. pp. 104–120.

George W. Randolph

George Wythe Randolph	
3rd Confederate States Secretary of War	
In office March 24, 1862 - November 15, 1862	
President	Jefferson Davis
Preceded by	Judah P. Benjamin
Succeeded by	James Seddon
Personal details	
Born	March 10, 1818 Charlottesville, Virginia, U.S.
Died	April 3, 1867 (aged 49) Charlottesville, Virginia, U.S.
Political party	Democratic
Spouse(s)	Mary Elizabeth Adams
Profession	Politician, Lawyer
Religion	Episcopalian

George Wythe Randolph (March 10, 1818 - April 3, 1867) was a lawyer, planter, and Confederate general. He served for eight months in 1862 as the Confederate States Secretary of War during the American Civil War, when he reformed procurement, wrote the conscription law, and strengthened western defenses. He was President Thomas Jefferson's youngest grandson by his daughter Martha Jefferson Randolph.

Biography

Randolph was born in 1818 at Monticello near Charlottesville, Virginia, to Martha Jefferson Randolph, the daughter of U.S. President Thomas Jefferson, and Thomas Mann Randolph Jr., a descendant of Pocahontas and John Rolfe. Their youngest son, he was named in honor of George Wythe, a signer of the Declaration of Independence and law professor of his grandfather Thomas Jefferson. He was also related to Edmund Randolph, who served in George Washington's cabinet as the first Attorney General of the United States, as well as colonist William Randolph through both his mother's and father's sides of the family.

Randolph briefly attended preparatory schools in Cambridge, Massachusetts and Washington, DC, where his mother sent him for distance from family troubles. His father had incurred much debt. He served as a midshipman in the United States Navy and began attending the University of Virginia while in the service.

Marriage and family

On April 10, 1852, he married the young widow Mary Elizabeth Adams Pope (1830-1871). They had no children.[163]

Career

After studying at the University of Virginia, Randolph "read the law" with an established firm and was admitted to the bar in 1840. He practiced law in Charlottesville, Virginia, and he and Mary lived at his plantation of Edgehill. They moved to the capital of Richmond in 1849. He became active in the community as well as having his law practice. He founded the Richmond Mechanics' Institute and was an officer in the Virginia Historical Society.[164]

As the Confederacy formed after southern states' secession, the United States divided into two hostile camps and the sections moved toward open conflict. A special delegation, composed of Randolph, William B. Preston and Alexander H.H. Stuart, traveled to Washington, D.C. where they met President Abraham Lincoln on April 12, 1861. Finding the President firm in his resolve to hold the Federal forts in the South, the three men returned to Richmond on April 15.[164]

Randolph was commissioned a major in the Confederate Army, and later served as a colonel of the artillery in the Battle of Big Bethel. He was promoted to brigadier general on February 12, 1862. Mary Randolph was active in the Richmond Ladies Association, which organized welfare and relief for the war effort.[164]

Randolph was appointed by Jefferson Davis as Secretary of War on March 18, 1862, and he took office on March 24, 1862. He helped reform the department, improving procurement and writing a conscription law similar to one he had created for Virginia. He was most well known for his strengthening the Confederacy's western and southern defenses, but came into conflict with Jefferson Davis over this. With weakening health due to tuberculosis (TB), he resigned on November 17, 1862.[164]

Post-Civil War

In 1864, Randolph took his family to exile in Europe, staying in England and France. They returned to Virginia in 1866. He died of TB in March 1867 at his Edgehill plantation.[164] He is buried at Monticello in the Jefferson family graveyard.

Legacy and honors

- Randolph was portrayed on the $100 bill printed by the Confederate States of America.

Further reading

- Daniels, Jonathan. *The Randolphs of Virginia: America's Foremost Family*, Garden City, New York: Doubleday, 1972.
- Janney, Caroline E. *Burying the Dead but Not the Past: Ladies' Memorial Associations and the Lost Cause*, Chapel Hill: University of North Carolina Press, 2008.
- Shackelford, George. *George Wythe Randolph and the Confederate Elite*, Athens, Georgia and London: University of Georgia Press, 1988.

External links

- "George W. Randolph"[165]. Find a Grave. Retrieved 2008-02-13.

James Seddon

James Alexander Seddon	
4th Confederate States Secretary of War	
In office November 21, 1862 - February 5, 1865	
President	Jefferson Davis
Preceded by	George W. Randolph
Succeeded by	John C. Breckinridge
Personal details	
Born	July 13, 1815 Falmouth, Virginia, U.S.
Died	August 19, 1880 (aged 65) Goochland County, Virginia, U.S.
Political party	Democratic
Spouse(s)	Sarah Bruce Seddon
Profession	Politician, Lawyer

James Alexander Seddon (July 13, 1815 - August 19, 1880) was an American lawyer and politician who served two terms in the U.S. Congress as a member of the Democratic Party. He was appointed Confederate States Secretary of War by Jefferson Davis during the American Civil War.

Biography

Seddon was born in Falmouth, Stafford County, Virginia. He was a descendant of William Alexander, Earl of Stirling. Due to frail health, he was educated primarily at home and became self-taught as a youth. At the age of twenty-one, Seddon entered the law school of the University of Virginia, graduating and settling in Richmond, where he established a successful law practice.

In 1845, he was nominated by the Democratic Party for Congress and was easily elected. Two years later, he was renominated, but declined due to platform differences with the party. In 1849, Seddon was reelected to Congress, serving from December 1849 until March 1851. Owing to poor health, he declined another nomination at the end of his term and retired to "Sabot Hill," his estate on the James River above Richmond.

Seddon attended the peace convention held in Washington, D.C., in 1861, which attempted to devise a means of preventing the impending civil war. Later in the same year, he attended the Provisional Confederate Congress. President Davis named him as the Secretary of War, a post he held until January 1, 1865, when he retired from public life to his country estate.

External links

- James Seddon[166] at the *Biographical Directory of the United States Congress*
- "James Seddon"[167]. Find a Grave. Retrieved January 12, 2010.
- James Seddon biography at Spartacus[168]
- James Seddon biography at the Confederate States War Department[169]

John C. Breckinridge

John C. Breckinridge	

1865-1875 photograph of John C. Breckinridge, attributed to Mathew Brady or Levin Handy. Scanned from original negative and retouched.	
14th Vice President of the United States	
In office March 4, 1857 - March 4, 1861	
President	James Buchanan
Preceded by	William R. King
Succeeded by	Hannibal Hamlin
5th Confederate States Secretary of War	
In office February 6, 1865 - May 10, 1865	
President	Jefferson Davis
Preceded by	James A. Seddon
Succeeded by	*Office abolished*
United States Senator from Kentucky	
In office March 4, 1861 - December 4, 1861	
Preceded by	John J. Crittenden
Succeeded by	Garrett Davis
Member of the U.S. House of Representatives from Kentucky's 8th district	
In office March 4, 1851 - March 3, 1855	
Preceded by	Charles Morehead
Succeeded by	Alexander Keith Marshall
Personal details	

Born	January 16, 1821 Lexington, Kentucky
Died	May 17, 1875 (aged 54) Lexington, Kentucky
Political party	Democratic
Spouse(s)	Mary Cyrene Burch Breckinridge
Alma mater	Centre College, College of New Jersey (now Princeton University), Transylvania University
Signature	
Military service	
Service/branch	Confederate States Army
Years of service	1861 - 1865
Rank	Major General
Battles/wars	Mexican-American War American Civil War

John Cabell Breckinridge (January 16, 1821 - May 17, 1875) was an American lawyer and politician. He served as a U.S. Representative and U.S. Senator from Kentucky and was the 14th Vice President of the United States (1857-1861), to date the youngest vice president in U.S. history, inaugurated at age 36.

In the 1860 presidential election, he ran as one of two candidates of the fractured Democratic Party, representing Southern Democrats. Breckinridge came in third place in the popular vote, behind winner Abraham Lincoln, a Republican, and Stephen Douglas, a Northern Democrat, but finished second in the Electoral College vote.

Following the outbreak of the American Civil War, he served in the Confederate States Army as a general and commander of Confederate forces prior to the 1863 Siege of Port Hudson, Louisiana, and of the young Virginia Military Institute cadets, at the 1864 Battle of New Market in Lexington, Virginia. He also served as the fifth and final Confederate Secretary of War.

A member of the prominent Breckinridge family of Kentucky, John C. Breckinridge was the grandson of John Breckinridge (1760-1806), who served as a Senator and Attorney General. He was also the father of congressman and diplomat Clifton Rodes Breckinridge and the great-grandfather of actor John Cabell "Bunny" Breckinridge.

Figure 24: *John C. Breckinridge in his younger years.*

Early life and education

Breckinridge was born at Cabell's Dale near Lexington, Kentucky, to Joseph Cabell Breckinridge and Mary Clay Smith. He graduated from Centre College in Danville, Kentucky in 1839 and later attended the College of New Jersey (now Princeton University). He then studied law at Transylvania University in Lexington and was admitted to the bar in 1840.

Legal, military, and political career in the antebellum period

He moved to Burlington, Iowa, but soon returned to Lexington and commenced the practice of law there. He was married to Mary Cyrene Burch on December 12, 1843, in Georgetown, Kentucky. In 1847 and 1848, during the Mexican-American War, Breckinridge was a major of the 3rd Kentucky Volunteers.

Breckinridge was a member of the Kentucky House of Representatives in 1849 as a Democrat. He was then elected to the Thirty-second and Thirty-third Congresses (March 4, 1851 - March 4, 1855). He did not run for reelection and, instead, was nominated as Minister to Spain by President Franklin Pierce but declined. He was elected Vice President of the United States in 1856 on the Democratic ticket with James Buchanan as president. He was the youngest Vice President in U.S. history, elected at the age 35, the minimum age required under the United States Constitution.

Breckinridge was an unsuccessful candidate for president in the 1860 election. Nominated by the Southern faction of the split Democratic Party, he was supported by incumbent Democratic president Buchanan and ran on a pro-slavery platform. The race put Breckinridge at odds with his uncle, Robert Jefferson Breckinridge, who had supported Lincoln.

Far from expectant of victory, in a letter to Varina Davis, Breckinridge bemoaned "I trust I have the courage to lead a forlorn hope." In a four-way contest, he came in third in the popular vote, with 18.1%, but second in the Electoral College, winning the states of the Deep South as well as the border states of Maryland and Delaware.

However, Breckinridge received almost no support in the most of the Northern states (which Lincoln swept except for split electoral votes from New Jersey going to Douglas and Lincoln) but, as the candidate of the Buchanan faction, did outpoll Douglas in Pennsylvania and won Delaware and received some support comparable to Douglas in Connecticut. Breckinridge lost to Douglas in Missouri and lost to Constitutional Union Party nominee John Bell in Virginia, Bell's home state of Tennessee, and even Breckinridge's own home state of Kentucky.

Despite losing the presidency, he was elected the same year to the United States Senate by the Kentucky Legislature. He served from March 4, 1861, and, as the outgoing vice president, swore in Lincoln's vice president, Hannibal Hamlin.

Despite the secession of the Southern states and the formation of the Confederate States of America, Breckinridge remained in the Senate until he was expelled by resolution on December 4, 1861, for supporting the South; ten Southern Senators had been expelled earlier the same year. Fearing arrest, he fled to the Confederacy. Unlike other Confederate leaders, such as Robert E. Lee, who claimed obeisance to the will of their states, Breckinridge broke with his state after the Kentucky Legislature voted to remain in the Union.

Civil War

Breckinridge entered the Confederate States Army during the American Civil War as a brigadier general and soon became a major general, originally commanding the 1st Kentucky Brigade, nicknamed the Orphan Brigade because its men felt orphaned by Kentucky's state government, which remained loyal to the Union. He fought in many battles in the Western Theater, beginning with the Battle of Shiloh, in which he was wounded. He served as an independent commander in the lower Mississippi Valley, securing Confederate control of the area by taking Port Hudson.

Breckinridge developed an intense personal dislike of General Braxton Bragg, the commander of the Army of Tennessee. He considered him incompetent, a point of view shared by many other Confederate officers. Furthermore, Breckinridge felt that Bragg was unfair in his treatment of Kentucky troops in Confederate service, such as the Orphan Brigade. Throughout the war, Breckinridge felt a strong personal need to see to the welfare of his fellow Kentuckians. For his part, Bragg despised Breckinridge and tried to undermine his career with accusations that he was a drunkard. At the Battle of Stones River in Murfreesboro, Tennessee, Bragg ordered Breckinridge's division to launch a near-suicidal attack on the Union lines on January 2, 1863. Breckinridge survived the attack, but his division suffered heavy casualties. Breckinridge was devastated by the disaster; he lost nearly one-third of his Kentucky troops, primarily the Orphan Brigade. As he rode among the survivors, he cried out repeatedly, "My poor Orphans! My poor Orphans."

Breckinridge continued to fight with Bragg's army, figuring prominently in the Confederate assaults on the second day, September 20, 1863, of the Battle of Chickamauga, and in the unsuccessful defense of Missionary Ridge in Chattanooga, November 25, 1863.

In early 1864, Breckinridge was brought to the Eastern Theater and put in charge of Confederate forces in the Shenandoah Valley. He defeated a superior Union force at the Battle of New Market, which included the famous charge of cadets from the Virginia Military Institute. Shortly thereafter, Breckinridge reinforced Robert E. Lee's Army of Northern Virginia and played an important role in the Battle of Cold Harbor, where his troops repulsed a powerful Union attack.

In the summer, Breckinridge participated in Lt. Gen. Jubal Early's Raid on Washington, moving north through the Shenandoah Valley and crossing into Maryland. He fought at the Battle of Monocacy in early July and was with Early when the Confederate force probed the defenses of Washington, D.C.. Since Lincoln was watching the fight from the ramparts of Fort Stevens, this was only time in American history when two former opponents in a presidential election faced one another across battle lines.

Following his service with Early's command, Breckinridge took command of Confederate forces in southwestern Virginia in September, where Confederate forces were in great disarray. He reorganized the department and led a raid

Figure 25: *Breckinridge as brigadier general*

Figure 26: *Breckinridge's statue at the Lexington History Center*

into northeastern Tennessee. Following a victory outside of Saltville, Breckinridge discovered that some Confederate troops had killed scores of black Union soldiers of the 5th United States Colored Cavalry the morning after the battle, an incident that shocked and angered him. He attempted to have the commander responsible, Felix Huston Robertson, arrested and put on trial, but was unable to achieve this before the Confederacy disintegrated.

In early 1865, Breckinridge was made Confederate States Secretary of War, a post he would hold until the end of the war. Breckinridge saw that further resistance on the part of the Confederacy was useless and worked to lay the groundwork for an honorable surrender, even while President Jefferson Davis fiercely desired to continue the fight.

During the chaos of the fall of Richmond in early April 1865, Breckinridge saw to it that the Confederate archives, both government and military, were not destroyed but rather captured intact by the Union forces. By so doing, he ensured that a full account of the Confederate war effort would be preserved for history. Breckinridge went with Davis during the flight from Virginia as the Confederacy collapsed, while also assisting General Joseph E. Johnston in his surrender negotiations with William T. Sherman at Bennett Place. Breckinridge continued to try to persuade Davis that further resistance would only lead to greater loss of life, but he also felt honor bound to protect the President from harm. Eventually, the two became separated in the confusion of the journey.

Postbellum career and legacy

Breckinridge feared that he would be put on trial for treason by the United States government and resolved to flee the country. He and a small band sailed from Florida in a tiny boat to reach safety in Cuba. He continued to the United Kingdom, Canada, and the United Kingdom again. He returned to Lexington, Kentucky, in March 1869 after being granted amnesty, and resumed the practice of law. While turning down suggestions that he become active in politics again, he spoke out strongly against the Ku Klux Klan. He became vice president of the Elizabethtown, Lexington, and Big Sandy Railroad Company. He died in Lexington of complications from cirrhosis[170] and was interred in Lexington Cemetery.

Breckinridge had ample reason to fear charges of treason; in 1863, premature rumors of his death prompted the *New York Times* to print a quite vituperative obituary arguing that Kentucky's decision to stay in the Union denied Breckinridge the notion of states' rights to justify his siding with the Confederacy.[171]

The towns of Breckenridge, Colorado; Breckenridge, Minnesota; Breckenridge, Missouri; and Breckenridge, Texas, were named in honor of the Vice

Figure 27: *John Breckinridge in his postbellum years.*

Figure 28: *Breckinridge's Gravestone*

President (despite the different spelling). The Colorado town deliberately changed the spelling of its name when its namesake joined the Confederacy.[172,173,174,175]

Breckinridge was the first Sovereign Grand Inspector General of the Ancient and Accepted Scottish Rite of Freemasonry in Kentucky.

A memorial to Breckinridge was placed on the Fayette County Courthouse lawn (now known as Cheapside Park) in Lexington in 1887. In 2009, the monument was relocated closer to Main Street as part of a reworking of Cheapside Park.

References

- Eicher, John H., and David J. Eicher. *Civil War High Commands*. Stanford, CA: Stanford University Press, 2001. ISBN 0-8047-3641-3.
- Woodworth, Steven E. *Jefferson Davis and His Generals: The Failure of Confederate Command in the West*. Lawrence: University Press of Kansas, 1990. ISBN 0-7006-0461-8.
- John C. Breckinridge[176] at the *Biographical Directory of the United States Congress* Retrieved on 2008-02-13

External links

- New York *Times* premature obituary[177]
- *Biographical sketches of Hon. John C. Breckinridge, Democratic nominee for president : and General Joseph Lane, Democratic nominee for Vice President*[178]
- John Cabell Breckinridge[179] at Find a Grave

Secretary of the Treasury: Memminger, Trenholm, Reagan**

Christopher Memminger

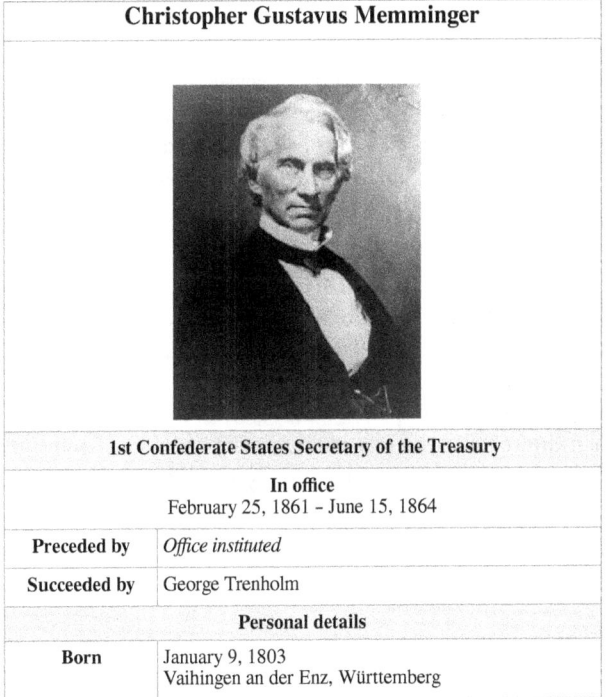

Christopher Gustavus Memminger	
1st Confederate States Secretary of the Treasury	
In office February 25, 1861 – June 15, 1864	
Preceded by	Office instituted
Succeeded by	George Trenholm
Personal details	
Born	January 9, 1803 Vaihingen an der Enz, Württemberg

Died	March 7, 1888 (aged 85) U.S.
Political party	Democratic
Spouse(s)	Mary Wilkinson Memminger
Profession	Politician, Lawyer
Religion	Episcopalian

Christopher Gustavus Memminger (January 9, 1803 - March 7, 1888) was a prominent political leader and the first Secretary of the Treasury for the Confederate States of America.

Early life and career

Memminger was born in Vaihingen an der Enz, Germany (in what was then the Duchy of Württemberg). His father, Gottfried Memminger, was a military officer who died in combat a month after his son's birth. His mother, Eberhardina Kohler Memminger, immigrated to Charleston, South Carolina, in the United States but died of yellow fever in 1807. Christopher was placed in an orphanage.[180]

Memminger's fortunes changed when, at the age of eleven, he was taken under the care of Thomas Bennett, a prominent lawyer and future Governor. Memminger was quite intelligent and entered South Carolina College at the age of 12 and graduated second in his class at 16. Memminger passed the bar in 1825 and became a successful lawyer. He married Mary Wilkinson in 1832.

He was a leader of the opponents during the nullification excitement. He published *The Book of Nullification* (1832-33) which satirized the advocates of the doctrine in biblical style.[181] He entered state politics and served in the South Carolina state legislature from 1836 to 1852 and 1854 to 1860, where for nearly twenty years he was the head of the finance committee.[182] Memminger was a staunch advocate of education and helped give Charleston one of the most comprehensive public school systems in the country.[183] In 1859, after John Brown's raid, he was commissioned by South Carolina to consult with other delegates in Virginia as to the best method of warding off attacks of abolitionists.[184]

Civil War

Memminger was considered a moderate on the secession issue, but after Lincoln's election, Memminger decided secession was necessary. When South Carolina seceded from the United States in 1860, Memminger was asked to

Figure 29: *The original Confederate Cabinet. L-R: Judah P. Benjamin, Stephen Mallory, Christopher Memminger, Alexander Stephens, LeRoy Pope Walker, Jefferson Davis, John H. Reagan and Robert Toombs.*

write the *Declaration of the Immediate Causes Which Induce and Justify the Secession of South Carolina from the Federal Union* which outlined the reasons for secession. When other states also seceded, Memminger was selected as a South Carolina delegate to the provisional congress which formed the Confederate States of America, and was the chairman of the committee which drafted the Confederate Constitution. The twelve-man committee produced a provisional constitution in only four days.

When Jefferson Davis formed his first cabinet, Memminger was chosen as Secretary of the Treasury on February 21, 1861. It was a difficult task, in view of the financial challenges facing the Confederacy. Memminger attempted to finance the government initially via bonds and tariffs (and confiscation of gold from the United States Mint in New Orleans), but soon found himself forced to more extreme measures such as income taxation and fiat currency. Memminger had been a supporter of hard currency before the war, but found himself issuing increasingly devalued paper money, which by war's end was worth less than two percent of its face value in gold.

Resignation

Memminger resigned his post as Secretary of the Treasury on July 18, 1864 and was replaced by fellow South Carolinian George Trenholm. Memminger returned to his summer residence in Flat Rock, Henderson County, North Carolina. In the post-war years, Memminger returned to Charleston, received a presidential pardon in 1866, and returned to private law practice and business investment. He also continued his work on developing South Carolina's public education system and was voted to a final term in the state legislature in 1877.

Legacy

Memminger was featured on the Confederate $5.00 bill.[185]

Bibliography

- Patrick, Rembert W. (1944). *Jefferson Davis and His Cabinet*. Baton Rouge: Louisiana State University Press. pp. 205-234.
- Schwab (1901). *The Confederate States of America, 1861-65: A Financial and Industrial History of the South During the Civil War*. New York.

George Trenholm

2nd Confederate States Secretary of the Treasury	
George Alfred Trenholm	
In office July 18, 1864 – April 27, 1865	
Preceded by	Christopher Memminger
Succeeded by	John Henninger Reagan
Personal details	
Born	February 25, 1807 Charleston, South Carolina, U.S.
Died	December 9, 1876 (aged 69) Charleston, South Carolina, U.S.
Political party	Democratic
Profession	Politician

George Alfred Trenholm (February 25, 1807 – December 9, 1876) was a prominent politician in the Confederate States of America and served as the Secretary of the Treasury during its final year.

Biography

George Alfred Trenholm was born in Charleston, South Carolina. When his father, William Trenholm, died, George left school early. He went to work for a major cotton broker, John Fraser and Company in Charleston. By 1853 he was head of the company, and by 1860 was one of the wealthiest men in the United States. He had interests in steamships, hotels, cotton, plantations, and slaves; he was also director of the Bank of Charleston and of a South Carolina railroad. When the Civil War broke out, John Fraser and Company became the Confederate government's overseas banker and financed its own fleet of blockade runners.[186] One of these may have been the SS Georgiana, which sunk in a naval action near Charleston in March 1863. Christopher Memminger used Trenholm as an unofficial adviser throughout his own term as Secretary of the Treasury; Trenholm was appointed to that post on July 18, 1864. He was a more charismatic figure than his predecessor and this helped him with the press and with Congress.[187]

Trenholm fled Richmond with the rest of the government in April, 1865 and went south as far as Fort Mill, South Carolina. Due to illness he asked President Davis to accept his resignation, which Davis accepted with his thanks on April 27, 1865.[188] He was later briefly imprisoned at Fort Pulaski near Savannah, Georgia.[189]

Bibliography

- Bulloch, James D. (2001). *The Secret Service of the Confederate States in Europe*. New York: Random House International. ISBN 0679-64022-3.
- Nepveux, Ethel Trenholm Seabrook (1973). *George Alfred Trenholm and the Company That Went to War*. Anderson, South Carolina: The Author. ISBN 0-9668843-1-0.
- Nepveux, Ethel Trenholm Seabrook (1999). *George A. Trenholm, Financial Genius of the Confederacy*. Anderson, South Carolina: The Author. ISBN 0-9668843-1-0.
- Patrick, Rembert W. (1944). *Jefferson Davis and His Cabinet*. Baton Rouge: Louisiana State University Press. pp. 234–243.
- Spence, E. Lee (1995). *Treasures of the Confederate Coast: The "Real Rhett Butler" & Other Revelations*. Miami: Narwhal Press. ISBN 1886391017.
- Spencer, Warren F. (1983). *The Confederate Navy In Europe*. University, Alabama: University of Alabama Press. ISBN 0-8173-0861-X.

Attorney General

Judah P. Benjamin

Judah P. Benjamin	
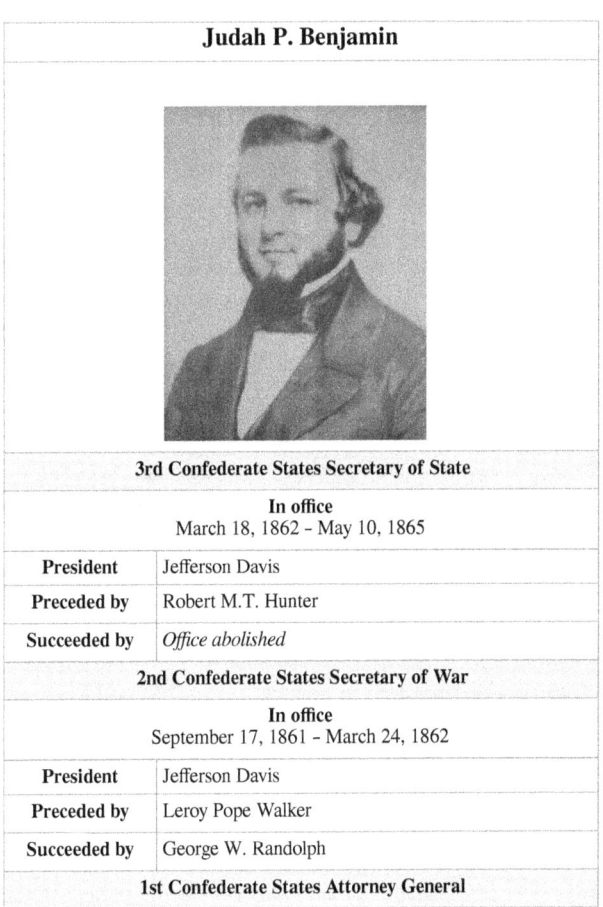	
3rd Confederate States Secretary of State	
In office March 18, 1862 - May 10, 1865	
President	Jefferson Davis
Preceded by	Robert M.T. Hunter
Succeeded by	*Office abolished*
2nd Confederate States Secretary of War	
In office September 17, 1861 - March 24, 1862	
President	Jefferson Davis
Preceded by	Leroy Pope Walker
Succeeded by	George W. Randolph
1st Confederate States Attorney General	

In office February 25, 1861 – September 17, 1861	
President	Jefferson Davis
Preceded by	*Office instituted*
Succeeded by	Thomas Bragg
Personal details	
Born	August 6, 1811 Christiansted, Saint Croix, West Indies
Died	May 6, 1884 (aged 72) Paris, France
Political party	Democratic
Spouse(s)	Natalie St. Martin
Children	Ninette Benjamin
Alma mater	Yale College
Profession	Politician, Lawyer
Religion	Judaism

Judah Philip Benjamin (August 6, 1811 – May 6, 1884) was an American politician and lawyer. Born a British subject in the West Indies, he moved to the United States with his parents and became a citizen. He later became a citizen of the Confederate States of America. After the collapse of the Confederacy, Benjamin moved to England, where he established a second legal career. In 1883 he retired and moved permanently to Paris, where his wife and daughter had lived for years. He died the following year.

During his career in U.S. politics, Benjamin was a member of the Louisiana House of Representatives; in 1852 he was elected by the state legislature to the US Senate from Louisiana; the second Jewish senator in U.S. history. Following the formation of the Confederate States of America in 1861, he was appointed by President Jefferson Davis to three different Cabinet posts in his administration. Benjamin was the first Jewish appointee to a Cabinet position in a North American government, and the first Jewish American to be seriously considered for nomination to the U.S. Supreme Court (he twice declined offers of nomination). Following his relocation to the United Kingdom, he became a distinguished barrister and was selected in 1872 as Queen's Counsel.

Family and early life

Judah Philip Benjamin was born a British subject in 1811 in Saint Croix, to Phillip Benjamin, an English Sephardic Jew, and his wife, Rebecca de Mendes, a Sephardic Jew from Spain.[190] This was during the period of the British occupation of the Danish West Indies (now U.S. Virgin Islands). His father was a first cousin and business partner of Moses Elias Levy, father of future Florida senator David Levy Yulee.[191]

He emigrated with his parents to the U.S. several years later, where the family first lived in North Carolina. By 1824 they had moved to Charleston, South Carolina, where his father was among the founders with Isaac Harby of the first Reform congregation in the United States, the "Reformed Society of Israelites for Promoting True Principles of Judaism According to Its Purity and Spirit." The formation of the congregation was of such interest that it was covered by the *North American Review,* a national journal of the time.[192]

As a youth, Benjamin attended Fayetteville Academy in North Carolina. At the age of fourteen, he entered Yale College. He left without completing the degree and read the law. In 1828 he moved to New Orleans, Louisiana to make his way, where he started clerking with a law firm as an alternative route to certification as an attorney.[193] He studied law and learned French to qualify to practice in Louisiana. He was admitted to the bar in 1833 at the age of 21. He entered private practice as a commercial lawyer.

Marriage and family

On February 16, 1833, the 22-year-old Benjamin married Natalie Bauché de St. Martin, the 16-year-old daughter of a prominent and wealthy New Orleans French Creole family. They were married in a Roman Catholic ceremony at the St. Louis Cathedral.[193] He became a slaveholder and soon established a sugar cane plantation in Belle Chasse, Louisiana. His plantation and legal practice both prospered.[194]

In 1842 the couple's only child, Ninette, was born. She was christened and raised as Catholic. In 1847 Natalie Benjamin took the girl and moved to Paris, where she remained for most of the rest of her life. Benjamin traveled each summer to France to see his wife and daughter.[194]

Political career

In 1842, Benjamin was elected to the lower house of the Louisiana State Legislature as a Whig. In 1845 he served as a member of the state Constitutional Convention. In 1850 he sold his plantation and its 150 slaves.

By 1852, Benjamin's reputation as an eloquent speaker with a subtle legal mind was sufficient to win him selection by the state legislature to the U.S. Senate. He was the second Jewish senator after David L. Yulee of Florida, who was elected by his state legislature in 1845.

Figure 30: *Judah Philip Benjamin, c. 1856*

The outgoing President, Millard Fillmore of the Whig Party, offered to nominate Benjamin, a Southerner, to fill a Supreme Court vacancy after the Senate Democrats had defeated Fillmore's other nominees for the post. The *New York Times* reported (on February 15, 1853) that "if the President nominates Benjamin, the Democrats are determined to confirm him." He was the first Jewish-American to be formally offered a Supreme Court appointment. Benjamin declined to be nominated. He took office as Senator on March 4, 1853. During his first year, he challenged another young Senator, Jefferson Davis of Mississippi, to a duel over a perceived insult on the Senate floor; Davis apologized, and the two began a close friendship.

Benjamin quickly gained a reputation as a great orator. In 1854 President Franklin Pierce offered him nomination to a seat on the Supreme Court, which he declined. He was a noted advocate of the interests of the South. According to the author Carl Sandburg, the abolitionist Benjamin Wade of Ohio said the Southern senator was "a Hebrew with Egyptian Principles", as he represented slaveholders.[195] Benjamin replied, "It is true that I am a Jew, and when my ancestors were receiving their Ten Commandments from the immediate Deity, amidst the thundering and lightnings of Mt. Sinai, the ancestors of my opponent were herding swine in the forests of Great Britain."[196]

By the next election, amid increasing regional tensions and divisions among Whigs over the issue of slavery, Benjamin had joined the Democratic Party;

Figure 31: *The original Confederate Cabinet, 1861. L-R: Judah P. Benjamin, Stephen Mallory, Christopher Memminger, Alexander Stephens, LeRoy Pope Walker, Jefferson Davis, John H. Reagan and Robert Toombs.*

in the South the party was dominated by the planter slaveholding elite. He was elected by the state legislature in 1858 to serve as US Senator. During the 34th through 36th Congresses, he was chairman of the Senate Committee on Private Land Claims. Benjamin resigned his seat on February 4, 1861, after Louisiana seceded from the Union.

Confederate statesman

Davis appointed Benjamin to be the first Attorney General of the Confederacy on February 25, 1861, remarking later that he chose him because he "had a very high reputation as a lawyer, and my acquaintance with him in the Senate had impressed me with the lucidity of his intellect, his systematic habits, and capacity for labor." Benjamin has been referred to as "the Brains of the Confederacy."[197]

In September 1861, he became the acting Secretary of War, and in November he was confirmed in the post. He became a lightning-rod for popular discontent with the Confederacy's military situation, and quarrelled with the Confederate Generals P.G.T. Beauregard and Stonewall Jackson. He had strong disagreements with Davis about how to conduct the war.

Worried about Confederate defenses in the West, Benjamin had urged foreign consuls in New Orleans to defend the city when attacked. He had no power to order them into Confederate military service. He ordered the seizure of fourteen privately owned steamers at New Orleans. The impressed vessels were strengthened with iron casings at the bow to be used as rams. The ships kept civilian crews. Each vessel had a single heavy gun to be used in the event it was attacked by the Union. The Confederacy allocated $300,000 to outfit these vessels.[198]

The military issues were highlighted by the Confederate's loss of Roanoke Island to the Union "without a fight" in February 1862. Roanoke's commander, Brig. Gen. Henry A. Wise was in desperate need of reinforcements when he was informed of the imminent Federal attack. He begged for some of the 13,000 men he knew were idle under the control of Maj. Gen. Benjamin Huger in nearby Norfolk, Va, but his pleas to Huger and Benjamin went unheeded. The heavily outnumbered Confederate force of some 2,500 surrendered and were taken prisoner after losing nearly a hundred of their number. (See Battle of Roanoke Island). Benjamin was held responsible for the loss (although he was carrying out Davis' priorities), and the public was outraged. Rather than reveal the pressing shortage of military manpower that had led to the decision to concede Roanoke, Benjamin accepted Congressional censure for the action without protest and resigned.

As a reward for Benjamin's loyalty, Davis appointed him as Secretary of State in March 1862. Benjamin arranged the Erlanger loan from a Paris bank to the Confederacy in 1863, which was the only significant European loan of the war.[199] In a round of "secondary diplomacy," he sent commercial agents to the Caribbean to negotiate opening ports in Bermuda, the West Indies, and Cuba to Confederate blockade-runners to maintain supplies, which the Union was trying to prevent. After mid-1863, the system was expanded and "brought rich rewards to investors, shipowners, and the Confederate Army."[200]

Benjamin wanted to draw the United Kingdom into the war on the side of the Confederacy, but it had abolished slavery years before and public opinion was strongly divided on the war. In 1864, as the South's military position became increasingly desperate, he publicly advocated a plan to emancipate and induct into the military any slave willing to bear arms for the Confederacy. Such a policy would have the dual results of removing slavery as the greatest obstacle in British public opinion to an alliance with the Confederacy, and easing the shortage of soldiers that was crippling the South's military efforts. With Davis' approval, Benjamin proclaimed, "Let us say to every Negro who wishes to go into the ranks, 'Go and fight — you are free." Robert E. Lee supported the scheme as well, but it faced stiff opposition from conservatives.

Figure 32: *Judah Philip Benjamin, c. 1860-1865)*

The Confederate Congress did not pass the measure until March 1865, by which time it was too late to salvage the Southern cause.

Benjamin is pictured on the CSA $2.00 bill.

Surrender of Confederacy

After Robert E. Lee's surrender, Judah P. Benjamin fled south with Jefferson Davis and the rest of his cabinet, but he left the group shortly before they reached Washington, Georgia, where they held their last meeting.[201] Benjamin is reported to have stayed in Ocala, Florida, with Solomon Benjamin, a relative,[202] before continuing south to Gamble Mansion in Ellenton. From there, assisted by the blockade runner Captain Archibald McNeill, who owned the plantation, as well as William Whitaker, Benjamin made it by sea to the Bahamas and then to England.[203] His escape from Florida to England was not without hardship. The small sponge-carrying vessel on which he left Bimini bound for Nassau exploded on the way, and he and the three crewmen had to be rescued by a British warship. His ship from the Bahamas to England caught fire on the way but managed to make it to port.[204] He was the only high-ranking Confederate politician to flee the country to avoid treason charges.[205]

Figure 33: *Benjamin's grave at Père Lachaise Cemetery in Paris*

In the immediate aftermath of the end of the war, Benjamin and Davis were rumored to have masterminded the assassination of Abraham Lincoln through the Confederate intelligence apparatus. According to Benjamin's biographer, Eli Evans, no evidence for this assertion has been found by historians.[196] Fearing that he could not receive a fair trial, Benjamin burned his papers, took brief refuge at Gamble Plantation on the west coast of southern Florida, and left for England under a false name. The historian Donald C. Simmons thinks that Benjamin may have considered joining his brother Joseph Benjamin, Colin J. McRae, the former Confederate Financial Agent in Europe, and other Confederates at New Richmond, British Honduras, in the Confederate settlements.[206]

Exile in England

From London in late 1865, Benjamin provided considerable financial assistance to several friends in the former Confederacy. Joan Cashin, the biographer of Varina Howell Davis, said that Benjamin gave the Davis family a gift of $12,000. The gift supported not only the Davis extended family but many of their relatives and friends during the early years of the Reconstruction era.

In June 1866, Benjamin was called to the bar in England, the beginning of his successful and eventually lucrative second career as a barrister, working in corporate law. In 1868, he published his *Treatise on the Law of Sale of*

Personal Property, which came to be regarded as one of the classics of its field. The work's current edition remains authoritative under the name *Benjamin's Sale of Goods*. He was influential in commercial law that supported the rise of Great Britain as an imperial power. In 1872 he was selected as Queen's Counsel.[190]

Benjamin retired in 1883 on his doctor's advice. He had earned $720,000 during his nearly two decades at the bar in London.[197] He moved to Paris, where his daughter Ninette and three grandchildren lived. He died there on May 6, 1884. He was interred at Père Lachaise Cemetery.[190]

Representation in fiction

- Robert D. Abrahams', *Mr. Benjamin's Sword* (1948) is juvenile historical fiction which covers the period of Benjamin's escape from Union forces after the loss of Richmond.
- Benjamin is featured as a politician and amateur detective in John Dickson Carr's *Papa La-Bas* (1968), a mystery set in New Orleans in 1858.
- Benjamin is a major character in the alternate history novel *Gray Victory* (1988) by Robert Skimin, taking place in 1866, in which the Confederacy has won independence. A mixed-race woman, who is a member of a secret abolitionist underground, has an affair with Benjamin.
- Benjamin, along with other historical figures, is a character in Harry Turtledove's alternate history novel *The Guns of the South* (1992).
- He is featured in *Southern Victory Series*, which chronicles an alternate history world after the South wins the Civil War. The Confederacy which Benjamin helped create is portrayed as an analog of Nazi Germany in the 1930s-1940s.
- In the 2004 mockumentary film *C.S.A.: The Confederate States of America*, Benjamin convinces France and Britain to side with the Confederacy, which wins the war.
- Benjamin figures prominently in the award-winning writer Dara Horn's short story "Passover in New Orleans" and her mystery novel, *All Other Nights* (2009). The story is a fictional account of an attempt to assassinate a New Orleans Jewish Confederate official before he can assassinate Lincoln.
- Benjamin is a character in a fictional mystery trilogy by the author and intelligence analyst W. Patrick Lang, a former US Army officer. His first two books of the trilogy are *The Butcher's Cleaver* (2007), and *Death Piled Hard* (2009).

Further reading

- Evans, Eli N., *Judah Benjamin: The Jewish Confederate*, New York: The Free Press, 1988.
- Judelson, Paul Alan. *Judah Philip Benjamin: Conservative Revolutionary*[207], Brown University Press, 1981
- Kahn, Eve M. (December 31, 2009). "Letters Reveal Doubts of Senator Judah Benjamin"[208]. *The New York Times*. Retrieved 9 January 2010.
- Korn, Bertram Wallace. *The Early Jews of New Orleans*[209], Waltham, MA: American Jewish Historical Society, 1969

External links

- Judah P. Benjamin[210] at the *Biographical Directory of the United States Congress*
- "Judah P. Benjamin"[211], Jewish Virtual Library
- "Judah P. Benjamin Home"[212], State historical marker at site of boyhood home in Wilmington, North Carolina, Historical Markers

Thomas Bragg

Thomas Bragg	
2nd Confederate States Attorney General	
In office November 21, 1861 – March 18, 1862	
Preceded by	Judah P. Benjamin
Succeeded by	Thomas H. Watts
Personal details	
Born	November 9, 1810 Warrenton, North Carolina
Died	January 21, 1872 (aged 61) Raleigh, North Carolina
Political party	Democratic
Profession	Politician, Lawyer

Thomas Bragg (November 9, 1810 – January 21, 1872) was a politician and lawyer who served as the 34th Governor of the U.S. state of North Carolina from 1855 through 1859. During the Civil War, he served in the Confederate States Cabinet. He was the older brother of General Braxton Bragg. They were direct descendants of Thomas Bragg (1579-1665) who was born in England and settled in the Virginia Colony.

Born in Warrenton, North Carolina, Bragg attended Warrenton Academy and later graduated from Captain Partridge's American Literary, Scientific & Military Academy. He was admitted to the bar in 1833 and commenced practice in Jackson, North Carolina. He was a member of the North Carolina General Assembly from 1842 to 1843 and became the prosecuting attorney for Northampton County. He successfully ran for Governor of North Carolina and served from 1855 to 1859. He then took a seat in the United States Senate, serving from 1859 until the start of the Civil War in 1861. He served as chairman of the Committee on Claims in the thirty-sixth congress. He was expelled for siding with the Confederacy. Confederate President Jefferson Davis appointed Bragg Attorney General of the Confederate States; he served from 1861 until his resignation in 1862. He continued to practice law until his death in 1872, and was also chairman of the central executive committee of the North Carolina Democratic Party (then called the Democratic-Conservative Party) as of 1870.[213] He was interred in Oakwood Cemetery in Raleigh, North Carolina.[214,215]

Bibliography

- Patrick, Rembert W. (1944). *Jefferson Davis and His Cabinet*. Baton Rouge: Louisiana State University Press. pp. 298-302.

Thomas H. Watts

	Thomas Hill Watts
	18th Governor of Alabama
	In office 1863-1865
Preceded by	John Gill Shorter
Succeeded by	Lewis E. Parsons
	Personal details
Born	January 3, 1819 Alabama Territory
Died	September 16, 1892 (aged 73) Montgomery, Alabama
Political party	Democratic

Thomas Hill Watts (January 3, 1819 - September 16, 1892) was the 18th Governor of the U.S. state of Alabama from 1863 to 1865, during the Civil War.

Watts was born in the Alabama Territory on January 3, 1819, the oldest of twelve children born to John Hughes Watts and Prudence Hill who had moved from Georgia to find the better lands of the frontier. Prepared for college at the Airy Mount Academy in Dallas County, Watts graduated with honors from the University of Virginia in 1840. He passed the bar examination the next year, and began practicing law in Greenville. In 1848 he moved his lucrative law practice to Montgomery. He also became a successful planter, owning 179 slaves in 1860.

Politically, Watts adopted a pro-Union stance during the 1850s, but subsequent developments made the depth of his beliefs questionable, for on the eve of the Civil War he played an important role in the secession of Alabama, and was one of the signers of the secession ordinance. Defeated by John Gill Shorter in an 1861 bid for governor, Watts organized the Seventeenth Alabama Regiment, but resigned later to become attorney general in President Jefferson Davis' cabinet.

In 1863 Watts was elected Governor of Alabama. Assuming office on December 1, he began an eighteen-month governorship at a time when impressment, the tax-in-kind, and other severe wartime economic measures had become most odious. Worthless Confederate money, lack of credit possibilities, irregular supplies of goods, impressment efforts that often amounted to pillage and plunder, and harsh (and unevenly applied) taxes-in-kind levied on agriculture convinced many people that they preferred the "Old Union" to the "new despotism". The need to raise troops for the defense of the state became more urgent. Appeals to the male population to form volunteer companies and appeals to the state legislature to reorganize the state's awkward two-class militia were met with unsurmountable resistance. Some critics of Watts thought he should concentrate on forcing deserters back into military service. The legislature's failure to act meant that the state, and the Confederacy, would not have an effective militia in the final critical months of the war. Furthermore, the Confederate Conscription Act of February 17, 1864, inaugurated a policy of conscription that inevitably led to conflict between the state and the Confederacy.

By September 1864 another turbulent issue confronted Governor Watts: the opening negotiations for peace. A faction in the Alabama House of Representatives introduced resolutions in favor of the negotiations. Governor Watts was also faced with rising desertion rates, states' rights issues including the controversy over the conscription of the cadets at the University of Alabama, the issue of which state civil officials were exempt from conscription, the defense of Mobile, blockade-running, and cotton trading with Europe. During the winter of 1864-65, Governor Watts had to deal with the increasing number of sacrifices demanded of his state, the breakdown of authority, the drain on war power, and an evaporating hope of victory, all of which contributed to the state's war weariness. Governor Watts was well aware of his ineffectiveness and unpopularity by this time and made no effort toward re-election, although he continued to talk optimistically about the military situation. Watts was Arrested for treason to the union in Union Springs on May 1, 1865. Governor Watts was released a few weeks later and returned to Montgomery.

He died twenty-seven years later on September 16, 1892 in Montgomery, Alabama.

References

- McMillan, Malcolm C. The Disintegration of a Confederate State, Three Governors and Alabama's Wartime Home Front, 1861-1865, 1986.
- http://www.archives.state.al.us/govs_list/g_wattst.html

George Davis (politician)

For the U.S. Representative from Illinois, see George R. Davis.

George Davis	
	Early photograph of Davis
4th Confederate States Attorney General	
In office January 2, 1864 – April 24, 1865	
President	Jefferson Davis
Vice President	Alexander Stephens
Preceded by	Thomas H. Watts
Succeeded by	*Office abolished*
Personal details	
Born	March 1, 1820 Wilmington, North Carolina, USA
Died	February 23, 1896 (aged 75) USA
Resting place	Oakdale Cemetery
Nationality	American
Political party	Democratic
Relations	Thomas Frederick Davis & Sarah Isabella Eagle (parents)
Alma mater	University of North Carolina at Chapel Hill

Profession	Law

George Davis (March 1, 1820 - February 23, 1896) was a Confederate States of America political figure and the last Confederate Attorney General, serving from 1864 to 1865.

He was not related to Confederate President Jefferson Davis.

Early life and career

Born near Wilmington, North Carolina, Davis attended the University of North Carolina at Chapel Hill, where he was valedictorian of the class of 1838. He subsequently studied law and was admitted to the bar in 1840. In 1848 he became general counsel of the Wilmington & Weldon Railroad. He held this position the rest of his life.

Political career

Davis was a delegate from North Carolina to the unsuccessful Washington Peace Conference of February 4-27, 1861.

After secession

Davis was a delegate to the Provisional Confederate Congress in 1861-1862, and was then elected to the Senate, where he served from 1862 to 1864. In December 1863, President Jefferson Davis appointed him Attorney General. He served in this position from January 2, 1864 until April 24, 1865, in the last days of the Confederacy.

After the war

Davis was captured by U.S. forces at Key West, Florida on October 18, 1865, and was imprisoned at Fort Hamilton in Brooklyn, N.Y. He spent several months at Fort Hamilton before being pardoned in 1866. He then returned to law practice in Wilmington.

Legacy

In World War II, the United States liberty ship SS *George Davis* was named in his honor.[216] A statue of Davis also stands in Wilmington, North Carolina.

Bibliography

- Patrick, Rembert W. (1944). *Jefferson Davis and His Cabinet*. Baton Rouge: Louisiana State University Press. pp. 104-120.

External links

- "George Davis (politician)"[217]. Find a Grave. Retrieved 2009-04-14.
- Short biography[218] csawardept.com

Postmaster General

John Henninger Reagan

John Henninger Reagan	
United States Senator from Texas	
In office March 4, 1887 - June 10, 1891	
Preceded by	Samuel B. Maxey
Succeeded by	Horace Chilton
Member of the U.S. House of Representatives from Texas's 2nd district	
In office March 4, 1883 - March 4, 1887	
Preceded by	David B. Culberson
Succeeded by	William H. Martin
Member of the U.S. House of Representatives from Texas's 1st district	
In office March 4, 1857 - March 4, 1861	

Preceded by	Lemuel D. Evans
Succeeded by	George W. Whitmore[1]
In office March 4, 1875 - March 4, 1883	
Preceded by	William S. Herndon
Succeeded by	Charles Stewart
3rd Confederate States Secretary of the Treasury	
In office April 27, 1865 - May 10, 1865	
Preceded by	George A. Trenholm
Succeeded by	Office abolished
1st Confederate States Postmaster General	
In office March 6, 1861 - May 10, 1865	
Preceded by	Office instituted
Succeeded by	Office abolished
Personal details	
Born	October 8, 1818 Sevier County, Tennessee
Died	March 6, 1905 (aged 86) Anderson County, Texas
Political party	Democratic
Spouse(s)	Edwina Moss Nelms Reagan
Profession	Politician, Lawyer, Surveyor
Religion	Methodist

John Henninger Reagan (October 8, 1818 - March 6, 1905), was a leading 19th century American politician from the U.S. state of Texas. A Democrat, Reagan resigned from the U.S. House of Representatives when Texas seceded from the Union and joined the Confederate States of America. He served in the cabinet of Jefferson Davis as Postmaster General. After the Confederate defeat, he called for cooperation with the federal government and thus became unpopular, but returned to public office when his predictions of harsh treatment for resistance were proved correct.[219][220][221]

Early life

Reagan was born in what is now Gatlinburg, Tennessee, to Timothy Richard and Elizabeth (Lusk) Reagan. He left Tennessee at nineteen and traveled to

Figure 34: *The original Confederate Cabinet. L-R: Judah P. Benjamin, Stephen Mallory, Christopher Memminger, Alexander Stephens, LeRoy Pope Walker, Jefferson Davis, John H. Reagan and Robert Toombs.*

Texas. He worked as a surveyor from 1839 to 1843, and then farmed in Kaufman County until 1851.[221] During the time he worked as a surveyor, he also served as a private tutor to the children of John Marie Durst.[222]

He studied law on his own and was licensed to practice in 1846, opening an office in Buffalo. The same year he was elected a probate judge in Henderson County and in 1847 he went to the state legislature, but was defeated for a second term in 1849. He was admitted to the bar in 1848 and practiced in both Buffalo and Palestine, Texas.[219]

Reagan was elected a district judge in Palestine, serving from 1852 to 1857. His efforts in defeating the American Party (Know-Nothings) led to his election to Congress in 1857 from First District.[219]

Reagan was a moderate and a supporter of the Union, but resigned from Congress on January 15, 1861 and returned home when it became clear that Texas would secede.[220] He participated in the secession convention that met at Austin on January 31, 1861. He was chosen a member of the Provisional Confederate Congress, but within a month he was appointed to his Cabinet post.

Civil War

President Jefferson Davis chose Reagan to head the new Confederate States of America Post-office Department. He was an able administrator, presiding over the only cabinet department that functioned well during the war. Despite the hostilities, the United States Post Office Department continued operations in the Confederacy until June 1, 1861, when the Confederate service took over its functions.[223] Reagan' sent an agent to Washington, D.C., with letters asking the heads of the United States Post Office Department's various bureaus to come work for him. Nearly all did so, bringing copies of their records, contracts, account books, etc. "Reagan in effect had stolen the U.S. Post Office," historian William C. Davis wrote. When President Davis asked his cabinet for the status of their departments, Reagan reported he had his up and running in only six weeks. Davis was amazed.

Reagan cut expenses by eliminating costly and little-used routes and forcing the railroads that carried the mail to reduce their rates. Despite the problems the war caused, his department managed to turn a profit, "the only post office department in American history to pay its own way," wrote William C. Davis. Reagan was the only member of the cabinet to oppose Robert E. Lee's offensive into Pennsylvania in June–July 1863. He instead supported a proposal to detach the First Corps of the Army of Northern Virginia to reinforce Joseph E. Johnston in Mississippi so that he could break the Siege of Vicksburg. Historian Shelby Foote noted that, as the only Cabinet member from west of the Mississippi, Reagan was acutely aware of the consequences of Vicksburg's capture.

When Davis abandoned Richmond on April 2, 1865, shortly before the entry of Army of the Potomac under George G. Meade, Reagan accompanied the president on his flight to the Carolinas. On April 27, Davis made him Secretary of the Treasury after George A. Trenholm's resignation and he served in that capacity until he, Davis, and Texas Governor Francis R. Lubbock were captured near Irwinville, Georgia on May 10.[220]

Reagan was imprisoned with Confederate Vice President Alexander Stephens at Fort Warren in Boston, where Reagan spent twenty-two weeks in solitary confinement.[221] On August 11, he wrote an open letter to his fellow Texans urging cooperation with the Union, renunciation of the secession convention, the abolition of slavery, and letting freed slaves vote. He warned of military rule that would enforce these policies if Texans did not voluntarily adopt them. For this, he was denounced by Texans. He was released from prison later that year and returned home to Palestine in December.[220]

Figure 35: *Reagan in his elder years*

Return to public life

To those who felt that the Reconstruction was unduly harsh, his prescience was hailed—he became known as the "Old Roman," a Texas Cincinnatus. He was part of the successful effort to remove Republican Edmund J. Davis from the governorship in 1874, after Davis attempted to illegally remain in office after he had lost the election. That year Reagan returned to the Congressional seat he held before the war, serving from March 4, 1875 to March 4, 1887. In 1875, he served in the convention that wrote a new state constitution for Texas. In Congress, he advocated federal regulation of railroads and helped create the Interstate Commerce Commission. He also served as the first chairman of the Committee on Post Offices and Post Roads. Though he had been elected to the Senate in 1887 (serving March 4, 1887 to June 10, 1891), he resigned to become chairman of the Railroad Commission of Texas at the behest of his friend, Governor James Stephen "Jim" Hogg, who had run on a platform of state regulation of railroads, and chaired it until 1903.[220][219]

Conscious of the importance of history, he was a founder of the Texas State Historical Association and attended reunions of Confederate veterans in his state. He wrote his *Memoirs, With Special Reference to Secession and the Civil War*, published in 1905, and died of pneumonia at his home in Palestine in Anderson County later that year, the last surviving member of the government

Figure 36:
*John H. Reagan
State Office Building*

of the Confederacy. Reagan was laid to rest in East Hill Cemetery Palestine Anderson County in Texas.[220][224]

Historian Ben H. Procter included Reagan in his list of the "four greatest Texans of the 19th century," along with Sam Houston, Stephen F. Austin, and James Stephen Hogg. Reagan County, Texas is named in his honor.[220]

Further reading

- Peter A. Branner. *The Organization of the Confederate Postoffice Department at Montgomery*. Montgomery, Alabama: The Author, 1960.
- August Dietz. *Confederate States Post-office Department*. Richmond, Virginia: Dietz Press, 1962.
- August Dietz. *The Postal Service of the Confederate States of America*. Richmond, Virginia: Dietz Printing, 1929.
- John Henninger Reagan. *Memoirs, With Special Reference to Secession and the Civil War*[225]. New York: Neale, 1905. (Reprinted subsequently)
- Ben H. Procter. *Not Without Honor*. Austin: University of Texas Press, 1962.

- Theron Wirenga, editor. *Official Documents of the Post-office Department of the Confederate States of America.* Holland, Michigan: The Editor, 1979. Two volumes.
- John Henninger Reagan[226] at the *Biographical Directory of the United States Congress* Retrieved on 2009-03-19

External links

- John Henninger Reagan[227] from the *Handbook of Texas Online*
- "John Henninger Reagan"[228]. Find a Grave. Retrieved 2009-03-19.
- John H. Reagan lineage[229] — Smokykin.com

Secretary of the Navy

Stephen Mallory

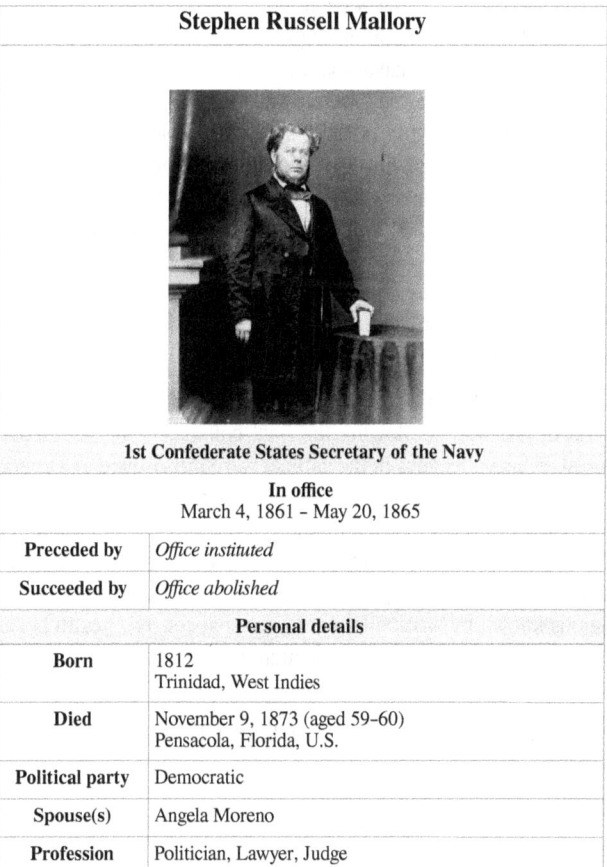

Stephen Russell Mallory	
1st Confederate States Secretary of the Navy	
In office March 4, 1861 – May 20, 1865	
Preceded by	*Office instituted*
Succeeded by	*Office abolished*
Personal details	
Born	1812 Trinidad, West Indies
Died	November 9, 1873 (aged 59–60) Pensacola, Florida, U.S.
Political party	Democratic
Spouse(s)	Angela Moreno
Profession	Politician, Lawyer, Judge

| Religion | Catholicism |

Stephen Russell Mallory (1812 – November 9, 1873) served in the United States Senate as, Senator (Democrat) from Florida from 1850 to the secession of his home state and the outbreak of the American Civil War. For much of that period, he was chairman of the Committee on Naval Affairs. This was a time of rapid naval reform, and he insisted that the ships of the United States Navy should be as capable as those of Great Britain and France, the foremost navies in the world at that time. He also wrote a bill and guided it through Congress that provided for compulsory retirement of officers who did not meet the standards of the profession.

Although he was not a leader in the secession movement, Mallory followed his state out of the Union. When the Confederate States of America was formed, he was named Secretary of the Navy in the administration of President Jefferson Davis. He held the position throughout the existence of the Confederacy. Because of indifference to naval matters by most others in the Confederacy, Mallory was able to shape the Confederate Navy according to the principles he had learned while serving in the US Senate. Some of his ideas, such as the incorporation of armor into warship construction, were quite successful and became standard in navies around the world; on the other hand, the navy was often handicapped by administrative ineptitude in the Navy Department. During the war, he was weakened politically by a Congressional investigation into the Navy Department for its failure in defense of New Orleans. After months of taking testimony, the investigating committee concluded that it had no evidence of wrongdoing on his part.

Mallory resigned after the Confederate government had fled from Richmond at the end of the war. Following the final collapse of the Confederacy, he and several of his colleagues in the cabinet were imprisoned and charged with treason. After more than a year in prison, the public mood had softened, and he was granted parole by President Andrew Johnson. He returned to Florida, where he supported his family in his final years by again practicing law. Unable to hold elective office by the terms of his parole, he continued to make his opinions known by writing letters to newspapers. His health began to deteriorate, although he was not incapacitated until the very end. He died on November 9, 1873.

He was the father of Stephen Russell Mallory, a U.S. Representative and Senator from Florida.

Early life

Mallory was born in Trinidad, British West Indies, in 1812.[230] His parents were Charles[231] and Ellen Mallory. His father was a construction engineer originally from Redding, Connecticut. He met and married the Irish-born Ellen Russell in Trinidad, and there the couple had two sons. The family moved to the United States and settled in Key West, Florida in 1820. Young Stephen was sent to school near Mobile, Alabama, but his education was interrupted by his father's death. His elder brother John also died about this time. To support herself and her surviving son, Ellen opened a boardinghouse for seamen. Then, she sent her son away for further schooling at a Moravian academy in Nazareth, Pennsylvania. Although he was for all of his life a practicing Catholic, he had only praise for the education he received at the academy. After about three years, his mother could no longer afford to pay his tuition, so in 1829 his schooling ended and he returned home.[232,233]

Adulthood in Florida

Young Mallory prepared for a profession by reading law in the office of Judge William Marvin.[234] Because of its geographical position, Key West was often sought as a port of refuge for ships caught in storms, and was for the same reason near frequent shipwrecks. Marvin was recognized as an authority on maritime law, particularly applied to laws of wreck and salvage, and Mallory argued many admiralty cases before him. He was reputed to be one of the best young trial lawyers in the state.[235]

His career prospering, in 1838 Mallory courted and wed Angela Moreno, member of a wealthy Spanish-speaking family living in Pensacola. Their marriage produced nine children, five of whom died young; daughters Margaret ("Maggie") and Ruby and sons Stephen R. Jr. ("Buddy") and Attila ("Attie") survived into adulthood. Buddy followed his father into politics, and he would eventually also serve as United States Senator from Florida.[236]

Mallory held a few minor public offices, beginning in 1832 with his selection as town marshal. One of his first paid positions was as Inspector of Customs, for which he earned three dollars per day. Later, President Polk appointed him Collector of Customs. Before his marriage, he joined the Army and took part in the Seminole War, 1835-1837. He also was elected judge for Monroe County for the years 1837-1845.[237]

In 1850, the sectional differences that eventually culminated in the Civil War led to a convention to be held in Nashville, Tennessee for the purpose of defining a common course of action for all Southern (slave-holding) states. Although Mallory had held no statewide offices, he was regarded as sufficiently powerful in the state Democratic Party to be chosen as an alternate delegate to the convention. Personal considerations kept him from attending, but he expressed his agreement with the purposes of the convention in a letter that was widely reprinted in the Florida newspapers.[238,239]

In the US Senate, 1850–1861

The term in office of Senator from Florida David Levy Yulee expired in 1850. He sought reappointment, but he had aligned himself too strongly with the Fire-eaters, and also had antagonized some commercial interests in the state. The moderates who favored working within the Union still dominated Florida politics, and they successfully sought to put Mallory in place of the radical Yulee. The selection process in the Florida state legislature was somewhat irregular, and Yulee protested, carrying his protest all the way to the Senate itself. That body determined that the Florida legislature had acted within its authority in certifying Mallory, and so he was seated.[240,241]

Senator from Florida

Much of what he did in the Senate can be described as the typical sponsorship of legislation that would benefit his state. With his sponsorship, the Senate passed a bill that would aid railroads in Florida, and another that would sell off some of the live oak reservations maintained by the Federal government for the Navy; both bills failed in the House of Representatives. He was more successful with bills aimed at prosecuting the ongoing campaign against the Seminole Indians, although the problem seems to have been overstated. His bills would provide compensation for persons who had suffered from the depredations of Indian raids, and would further the process of removing the aborigines from the state. He also introduced bills that provided for marine hospitals in port cities in Florida. None of this would have been considered exceptional for the era.[242]

Committee on Naval Affairs

Mallory was placed on the Senate Committee on Naval Affairs.[243] His assignment became significant when President Millard Fillmore in his Message to Congress of December 13, 1851, recommended Congressional action on two issues. First was the problem of what to do with ineffective officers in the Navy. At the time, promotion was based solely on seniority, and no policy existed for removing officers who could not or would not fulfill their duties. Second was the issue of discipline in the enlisted rates. The practice of flogging had been outlawed in the previous Congress, and many of the old captains believed discipline on their warships was deteriorating; they wanted a return to the old ways, or at least a reasonable substitute that would enable them to exert their authority.[244]

Mallory's first major speech in Congress was in favor of a return to flogging, which he argued was needed in order that a captain would be able to control his seamen in battle. His position was unpopular throughout the nation, and Congress refused to lift the ban.[245,246] His views on flogging, for good or ill, were forgotten when he turned his energies to the second of President Fillmore's proposals, that of reforming the officer corps of the Navy. He was by this time chairman of the Senate Committee on Naval Affairs,[247] and the law that Congress passed was recognized as coming from his hand. It established a Retirement Board of senior naval officers, who examined the qualifications of all other commissioned officers. Those who were deemed incapable or unworthy of their rank were placed on a retired list, the first compulsory retirement in the history of the US Navy. By most accounts, the board did its work creditably, but many of the officers who were adversely affected did not agree. Among those who were forced into early retirement was Matthew Fontaine Maury, too crippled to go to sea, but whose study of ocean currents formed the basis for the new science of oceanography. Maury and some of the other retirees enlisted other Senators to support their cases, and the debate was renewed. In the end, however, Mallory's views prevailed, a testimonial to his parliamentary skills. The enmity between Maury and Mallory lasted the remainder of their lives and distorted their performance in the Civil War, when both men sided with the South.[248]

Mallory's tenure on the Committee on Naval Affairs came during a time of great innovation in naval warfare. He kept abreast of developments in other navies, and he made sure that the US Navy would incorporate the latest thinking into its new ships. Britain and France, then the two foremost navies in the world, were in the process of converting their fleets from sail to steam, and from paddles to screws. In 1853, the committee recommended passage of a bill providing for the addition of six new screw frigates to the fleet; when delivered, some considered them to be the best frigates in the world. In 1857, his committee persuaded the Senate to authorize twelve sloops-of-war. These entered the navy beginning in 1858, on the verge of the Civil War.[249]

Another innovation that was being considered was that of armor. Mallory was here somewhat ahead of his time, enthusiastically supporting iron cladding for ships before the fledgling metals industry in the country could supply it in the requisite quantities. No armored vessels were commissioned while he was in the Senate, but whatever fault there was lay elsewhere. He spoke up for extending appropriations for an armored vessel that was intended for the defense of New York Harbor; named the Stevens Battery after its designer and builder Robert L. Stevens, it had been laid down in 1842 but was still incomplete in

1853, when Mallory gave his argument. His pleading was unsuccessful in that the Senate did not agree to continue funding the project, but in his supporting speech he expressed some of the principles that guided his thinking when he later became the Confederate Secretary of the Navy.[250]

Sectional crisis

Representing as he did a state in the Deep South, Mallory could hardly have avoided taking a public stance on the issues that were tearing the nation apart. The occasion arose when the Senate considered the admission of Kansas to the Union. Its Lecompton Constitution would allow slavery in Kansas, and citizens who were against extending the practice into new territories seized upon the widespread irregularities in the adoption procedure to oppose it. Senator Preston King of New York mounted a two-hour attack on the constitution and Southern policy in general, following which Mallory replied in what his biographers describe as "probably his most effective speech in the Senate."[251] One segment of his talk presented the rationale of the slave-holders in their unwillingness to accept majority rule. Addressing the question whether the constitution had been ratified by "the people," he said: "States have conferred, and may at any time confer, their whole political power on a minority. They may make disqualifications dependent upon the tenure of freehold estate, upon the payment of tax, upon militia duty, or upon the color of skin; but whoever the State chooses to confer her political authority upon, are the people." He foresaw the decline in relative power of the slave-holding states, although at this time he did not believe it would necessarily lead to secession. He concluded his remarks by a pledge to follow the South whatever happened: "It is not for me to indicate the path she [the South] may, in her wisdom, pursue; but, sir, ... my whole heart is with her, and she will find me treading it with undivided affections."[252]

Despite his willing adherence to the Southern position on the issues that were dividing the country, Mallory was not prominent in the secession movement. He advocated reconciliation almost up to the moment that Florida passed its ordnance of secession. That occurred on January 10, 1861, making Florida the third state (behind South Carolina and Mississippi) to leave the Union. On January 21, Mallory delivered his farewell speech in the United States Senate.[253]

In the days before Abraham Lincoln took office, parties in the seceding states disagreed over the proper course of action concerning the forts within their domains. In Florida, three forts remained in the possession of the United States Army: Fort Zachary Taylor at Key West, Fort Jefferson in the Dry Tortugas, and Fort Pickens near Pensacola.[254] Some of the most strident secessionists proposed that they be taken over immediately, by force if needed, beginning

Figure 37: *The original Confederate Cabinet. L-R: Judah P. Benjamin, Stephen Mallory, Christopher Memminger, Alexander Stephens, LeRoy Pope Walker, Jefferson Davis, John H. Reagan and Robert Toombs*

with Fort Pickens. Cooler heads hoped to avoid bloodshed and gain possession by negotiation; they made much of the conciliatory words of William H. Seward, already selected to be Secretary of State in the incoming administration. Mallory and Florida's other Senator, David L. Yulee, and the two Senators from Alabama sent telegrams to their respective governors urging caution. Other Southern Senators lent their support, and President-elect Jefferson Davis seemed to agree. In the end, the moderates won out, and no attack was made on Fort Pickens. Although Mallory was hardly alone, his political opponents later used his perceived pro-Union stance as an excuse to attack him.[255]

Confederate Secretary of the Navy: nomination and confirmation

The governmental structure of the newly-formed Confederate States of America was very much like that of the parent United States. The executive branch was partitioned into several departments, each headed by a secretary or equivalent who would advise the president. The constitution provided for a navy that would be directed by its own department, and President Jefferson Davis nominated Mallory to be Confederate States Secretary of the Navy. He was chosen for two principal reasons: first, he had extensive experience with nautical affairs, both in his boyhood home of Key West and later in Washington; and second, he was from Florida. In a bow to the principle of States' Rights, Davis had to spread representation in his cabinet around among the seceding states. Although the requirement of geographical representation sometimes meant that the occupant would not be the best person available, the selection process worked well in Mallory's case.[256]

Mallory's nomination as Secretary of the Navy was submitted to the Provisional Congress as soon as the act establishing a navy was passed. Despite his evident qualifications, it drew significant opposition; his detractors cited the Fort Pickens incident as evidence that he was not strongly pro-secession. Ultimately, however, he was confirmed.[257,258]

Naval organization and operations

As few other persons in the Confederate government were interested in naval matters, Mallory had almost free rein to shape the department, as well as the navy it controlled, according to his own views. The result was very much the product of his prior experience. The Department of the Navy was organized into separate offices, equivalent to the bureau system of the United States Navy; whereas the US Navy had five bureaus, the Confederate Navy had only four: Orders and Detail (dealing with personnel), Provisions and Clothing, Medicine and Surgery, and Ordnance and Hydrography.[259] Although there was no Office of Construction and Repair, its function was met by John L. Porter. Porter served as Chief Naval Constructor, without title from the start until the position was officially established in 1863, and thereafter with title until the end of the war.[260] A few other functions lay outside the bureau system: a small Marine Corps, a few men who were sent to Europe to acquire vessels there and who reported directly to Mallory, and a Torpedo Bureau.[261]

At the start, the Confederate Navy faced one of the problems that Mallory had encountered when he was chairman of the United States Senate Committee on Naval Affairs: an overabundance of high-ranking officers who were too old to go to sea. This came about because the Confederacy had created its navy by promising that men resigning from the US Navy would enter the CS Navy at their old rank. Hoping to avoid the stagnation that was the result of the former promotion process, Mallory proposed that promotion should depend solely on "gallant or meritorious conduct during the war."[262] His proposal was quickly made into law by the Confederate Congress. Still not completely satisfied, in 1863 Mallory initiated the creation of a Provisional Navy, which in effect established two officer corps. The officers whom Mallory or his advisers deemed incapable of combat were retained in the Regular Navy, while young and presumably more aggressive officers would transfer to the Provisional Navy. Officers for fighting ships would be drawn from the Provisional Navy, and they could be promoted without regard for seniority if they served with distinction.[263]

Mallory also was able to shape naval policy and doctrine. After viewing the disparity between the shipbuilding and other manufacturing facilities of the Confederacy and those of the Union, he set forth a fourfold plan for the navy:[264]

1. Send out commerce raiders to destroy the enemy's mercantile marine.

2. Build ironclad vessels in Southern shipyards for defensive purposes.

3. Obtain by purchase or construction abroad armored ships capable of fighting on the open seas.

4. Employ new weapons and techniques of warfare.

Attacks on Union commerce

From the start, one of the main efforts of the Confederate Navy was to counter the blockade of its ports by the Union Navy. Mallory believed that by attacking the merchant shipping that carried trade to Northern ports he could force his Union counterpart, Secretary of the Navy Gideon Welles, to divert his own small fleet to defend against the raiders. In the early days of the war, the Confederacy tried to enlist the services of private shipowners in the service by offering letters of marque and reprisal. Issuance of the letters was not in the purview of the Navy Department, but Mallory was aware of them and saw them as part of his plan. For several reasons, the privateers did not have the success that was hoped for. Although they ventured out throughout the war, they had only fleeting success, and that had ceased by the end of the first year.[265,266]

He was more directly involved in the activities of the commissioned raiders, ships of the Confederate States Navy that were sent out to destroy rather than capture enemy commerce. He first proposed their use as early as April 18, 1861. The first raider, CSS *Sumter*, avoided the Union blockade at New Orleans on June 30, 1861. From then until after the war was over, the small[267] group of raiders plundered Union shipping, inflicting damage on the American Merchant Marine that persists to the present day.[268] They failed of their primary purpose, however, because Welles maintained the Union blockade, and international trade continued as before, carried in ships flying foreign flags.[269,270]

Naval reform: ironclads

No other aspect of Mallory's tenure as Secretary of the Navy is better known than his advocacy of armored vessels. He argued that the Confederacy could never produce enough ships to compete with the industrial Union on a ship-by-ship basis. As he saw it, the South should build a few ships that were individually so far superior to their opponents as to dominate. In his words, "The perfection of a warship would doubtless be a combination of the greatest known ocean speed with the greatest known floating battery and power of resistance."[271] He hoped that armored warships would prove to be the "ultimate weapon." He did not anticipate that his opponents would also produce armored vessels, which rapidly became important parts of both navies. Furthermore, other navies, notably Great Britain and France, stepped up the conversions of their own fleets from wood to iron. Certainly the change was under way even before the Civil War broke out; his legacy consists in forcing the change to be made sooner than would otherwise have been done.[272]

The first ironclad to be created at Mallory's urging[273] was CSS *Virginia*. The burned and scuttled USS *Merrimack* had been raised at Gosport (Norfolk) Navy Yard, and an armored casemate built on her hull. For armament, she carried 12 guns. She was also fitted with an iron ram. On March 8, 1862, she attacked the Union fleet enforcing the blockade at Hampton Roads, on the James River near Norfolk. She sank two major Union warships (USS *Cumberland* and *Congress*), and menaced a third (*Minnesota*), which had grounded in the attempt to get into action. The damages she suffered were negligible. In that first day of the battle, she had demonstrated the basic validity of Mallory's belief that armored warships could destroy the best wooden ships and were almost impervious to damage in return.[274] As is well known, when *Virginia* returned to battle the next day intending to finish off *Minnesota*, she encountered the Union's *Monitor*. The two armored vessels fought inconclusively, demonstrating the flaw in Mallory's argument: an ultimate weapon is truly decisive only if one side does not have it.[275]

After *Virginia*, most other Confederate ironclads had at best limited success, and many were complete failures. Particularly embarrassing were four that were contracted to be built for service on the Mississippi River. Of the four, only one, CSS *Arkansas*, entered into combat in the way that was intended, with full crew and under steam. Of the others, *Tennessee* was destroyed on the stocks; *Mississippi* was hastily launched and then burned to avoid capture; and *Louisiana* was used merely as an ineffectual floating battery at the Battle of Forts Jackson and St. Philip, when the fate of New Orleans was decided, and she was then blown up rather than be surrendered. No parties in the Confederacy acquitted themselves well in the three losses, but Mallory must bear a large part of the blame. Poor administration is among the foremost reasons for the delays that hindered completion of the vessels. By failing to prioritize their construction, he allowed *Louisiana* and *Mississippi* to compete for scarce resources. Because he did not delegate responsibility, he was swamped with details of the construction of *Virginia* while letting problems concerning the other ships go unresolved. And because he accepted the role implicitly assigned to his service as secondary to the Army, the Navy had to work with only the materials and funds that were left over after the Army had satisfied its needs.[276]

Mission to Europe

The backward condition of shipyards in the seceding states convinced Mallory that he would have to look abroad to obtain the vessels that he thought would be able to challenge the US Navy. He selected two men as his primary representatives: James D. Bulloch and Lieutenant James H. North of the Confederate States Navy. North was a disappointment, but Bulloch proved to be one of the most effective agents for the Confederacy in Europe. He sought diligently and discreetly in England to acquire ships for the purposes of his government while working within or around the framework of the neutrality laws of the host nation.[277,278]

Four of the Confederate Navy raiders were purchased in Britain: CSS *Florida*, *Georgia*, *Shenandoah*, and above all *Alabama*. Probably Mallory would have liked to have more, but the record shows that the few that were commissioned were more than adequate.[279]

Efforts to purchase or have built ironclad warships were unsuccessful despite Bulloch's best efforts. Buying them was never seriously considered, as the Royal Navy would not care to give any of its best ships to a foreign power, no matter how favorably disposed. Contracts were made with private shipyards in both Britain and France to build rams[280] to Confederate naval specifications, but their ultimate purpose could not be disguised. They therefore directly violated the neutrality laws, and American (that is, Union) officials immediately informed the governments of their existence. For a while, Her Majesty's Government chose to turn a blind eye on developments, but the Union victories at Gettysburg and Vicksburg caused them to reconsider. On September 5, 1863, Ambassador Charles Francis Adams sent a message to Foreign Minister Lord John Russell informing him that the first of the ironclads was about to leave, and that "it would be superfluous in me to point out to your Lordship that this means war." The ship was not permitted to leave and was later seized for the Royal Navy. As the French government had implicitly agreed to follow Britain's lead concerning North America, all the contracts were voided.[281]

New weapons

The Civil War provided a testing ground for numerous innovations in warfare, and Mallory was in position to provide support for many of them. His advocacy of armored vessels has been described and is the development most closely associated with his name,[282] but he encouraged the development of several other weapons. For example, he favored the use of rifled guns, as opposed to the smoothbore muzzle loaders used in the Union Navy. The favored gun was a rifle designed by the head of his Office of Ordnance and Hydrography, Lieutenant John Mercer Brooke. The Brooke rifle gave Rebel gunners a qualitative advantage over their Yankee counterparts that persisted to the end of the war.[283]

The torpedo office, officially named the Submarine Battery Service,[284] developed underwater explosive devices, known as "torpedoes" at that time but as "mines" today. The office was initially led by Mallory's enemy Matthew Fontaine Maury, and later by Lieutenant Hunter Davidson. The first ship to be lost to mines was USS *Cairo*, on December 12, 1862.[285] Subsequently, more vessels of all types were lost in combat to mines and torpedoes than from all other causes combined.[286,287,288]

In Charleston Harbor, Army Captain Francis D. Lee, supported by General P. G. T. Beauregard, developed a small boat that would carry a spar torpedo. His craft, known as *David*, successfully exploded a torpedo against the side of USS *New Ironsides*, severely damaging her.[289] Later, the more famous *H. L. Hunley* used one of Lee's spar torpedoes to sink USS *Housatonic*, the first ship to be sunk by a submarine.[290] The Navy Department had not provided active support for Lee's experiments, but their successful result led to the use of spar torpedoes on ships throughout the fleet. (Less favorably for the Rebel cause, spar torpedoes were also immediately adopted by the Union Navy, and one was used in October 1864 to sink the ironclad CSS *Albemarle*.)[291]

Investigation of the Navy Department

The loss of New Orleans came as a tremendous shock to the Confederacy, and a spate of recriminations followed. Members of Congress, noting the failure of the ironclads, blamed the navy in particular, and suggested that there was no need for a separate Navy Department. Hoping to forestall such a proposal, Mallory was able to persuade the Congress instead to investigate the conduct of the department. Each house put five of its members on the investigating committee. The chairman, Senator Clement C. Clay, was known as one of Mallory's friends, as was Representative Ethelbert Barksdale. They were at least partially balanced by Representative Henry S. Foote, a persistent critic of secession and everything that the entire Davis administration had done.

Also weighing in against Mallory was Senator Charles M. Conrad, chairman of the Naval Affairs Committee, who was not a member of the investigating committee but who did appear as a prosecution witness. The committee continued to meet for more than six months, and ended with no finding of neglect or malfeasance.[292]

The investigation may have weakened Mallory politically and certainly diverted him from other duties, but it was not enough to drive him from office. Perhaps because there was no one to replace him and perhaps because he absorbed shafts that were aimed at the president, Davis retained him in the cabinet until the end of the war. After the surrender of Lee's army at Appomattox, Mallory remained with Davis and the other cabinet members as they fled deeper into the South, first to Danville, Virginia, then to Greensboro, North Carolina, Charlotte, Abbeville, South Carolina, and finally Washington, Georgia. There, Mallory submitted his resignation and went to La Grange, Georgia, where he was temporarily reunited with his wife and children.[293]

After the war

Capture and imprisonment

A large part of the population of the Northern states believed that the Davis government was somehow involved in the assassination of Abraham Lincoln, and although there was no evidence of their complicity, it was a political reality that had to be dealt with. One result was that the political radicals were able to force the government to prosecute those who had led the war against the Union. Mallory was one of the Confederate leaders who were charged with treason, among other things; on May 20, 1865, while he was still at La Grange, he was roused from his sleep at about midnight and taken into custody. From there he was taken to Fort Lafayette in New York Harbor, where he was confined as a political prisoner.[294]

For several months, the demand of the public for vengeance increased, so that Mallory feared that he would face the death penalty if convicted. However, no bill of particulars to specify precisely which of his acts constituted treason was ever presented, and it became increasingly clear that no one in the Confederate government was guilty of assassinating the former president. The period for extracting vengeance passed with no one put on trial, and hope was revived. From his prison cell, Mallory began to write letters in a personal campaign to gain release. He petitioned President Andrew Johnson directly, and enlisted the support of some of his former colleagues in the Senate. His wife Angela visited Washington and importuned President Johnson and other persons who had influence. Johnson was already quite lenient in granting pardons, and the popular clamor for harsh punishment began to recede by the end of the year.

On March 10, 1866, Johnson granted Mallory a "partial parole." Although he was no longer in jail, he was required to stay with his daughter in Bridgeport, Connecticut until he could take the oath of allegiance.[295]

Release and return to Florida

In June 1866, Mallory visited Washington, where he called on many of his old friends and political adversaries, including President Johnson and Secretary of War Edwin M. Stanton, who received him cordially. He got permission to return to Florida; his return was somewhat delayed by problems with his health, but on July 19 he arrived at his home in Pensacola.[296]

By the terms of his parole, Mallory was not permitted to hold public office, so he made a living by reopening his old law practice. Nominally excluded from politics, he managed to make his views known by writing letters and editorials for Florida newspapers. At first he urged acceptance of the reconstituted Union and acquiescence in the policies of Reconstruction, but he soon came out in opposition, particularly against black suffrage.[297]

He had long suffered occasional attacks of gout, and these continued to plague him in the postwar years. In the winter of 1871-1872 he began to complain of his heart, and his health began to deteriorate. Still, he remained active, and the end came rather quickly. He is said to have been "listless" on November 8, 1873, and that night he began to fail. On the morning of November 9 he died.[298] He was buried in St. Michael's Cemetery, Pensacola, Florida.

References

- Anderson, Bern, *By Sea and by River: The Naval History of the Civil War.* New York: Knopf, 1962; reprint, Da Capo Press, 1989.
- Durkin, Joseph T., *Confederate Navy Chief: Stephen R. Mallory.* Columbia, S.C.: University of South Carolina Press, 1987. ISBN 0872495183
- *Historical Times Illustrated Encyclopedia of the Civil War,* Patricia L. Faust, editor. New York: Harper & Row, 1986. ISBN 0061812617
- Hearn, Chester G., *The Capture of New Orleans, 1862.* Baton Rouge: Louisiana State University Press, 1995. ISBN 0807119458
- Luraghi, Raimondo, *A History of the Confederate Navy.* (tr. Paolo E. Coletta, *Marina del Sud: storia della marina confederate nella Guerra Civile Americana, 1861-1865.* Rizzoli, 1993.) Annapolis: Naval Institute Press, 1996. ISBN 1557505276
- Perry, Milton F., *Infernal Machines: The Story of Confederate Submarine and Mine Warfare.* Baton Rouge: Louisiana State University Press, 1965.

- Scharf, J. Thomas, *History of the Confederate States Navy from Its Organization to the Surrender of Its Last Vessel; Its Stupendous Struggle with the Great Navy of the United States, the Engagements Fought in the Rivers and Harbors of the South and upon the High Seas, Blockade-Running, First Use of Iron-Clads and Torpedoes, and Privateer History.* New York, Rogers & Sherwood, 1887.
- Simson, Jay W., *Naval Strategies of the Civil War: Confederate Innovations and Federal Opportunism.* Nashville, Tenn.: Cumberland House, 2001. ISBN 1581821956
- Still, William N., *Iron Afloat: The Story of the Confederate Armorclads.* Nashville: Vanderbilt University Press, 1971; reprint, Columbia, S.C.: University of South Carolina Press, 1985. ISBN 0872494543
- Tucker, Spencer C., *Handbook of 19th Century Naval Warfare.* Annapolis: Naval Institute Press, 2000. ISBN 1557503222
- Underwood, Rodman L., *Stephen Russell Mallory: a Biography of the Confederate Navy Secretary and United States Senator.* Jefferson, N.C.: McFarland & Co., 2005. ISBN 0786422998 (alk. paper)

External links

- Biographical Directory of the US Congress[299]
- ⓘ "Stephen Russell Mallory". *Catholic Encyclopedia.* New York: Robert Appleton Company. 1913.

* Judah Benjamin held 3 posts: Attorney General, War and State

** John Reagan held 2 posts: Postmaster General and Treasury

Appendix

References

[1] Foote, Shelby (1958). *The Civil War: A Narrative, Fort Sumter to Perryville*. New York: Random House. p. 3.
[2] Strode 1955, p. 230.
[3] Cooper 2008, pp. 1-5.
[4] Wiley, Bell I. (January 1967). "Jefferson Davis: An Appraisal". *Civil War Times Illustrated* **6** (1): 4-17.
[5] "Restoration of Citizenship Rights to Jefferson F. Davis Statement on Signing S. J. Res. 16 into Law" http://www.presidency.ucsb.edu/ws/?pid=29993. The American Presidency Project. Retrieved 2011-07-17.
[6] Strawbridge, Wilm K. (December 2007). "A Monument Better Than Marble: Jefferson Davis and the New South". *Journal of Mississippi History* **69** (4): 325-347.
[7] Collins 2005, p. 156.
[8] "Jefferson Davis' Loyalty". *The Meriden Daily Journal*: p. 1. May 14, 1887.
[9] "Jeff Davis Coming Around" http://query.nytimes.com/gst/abstract.html?res=9D01E0DE1730E633A25757C1A9639C94669FD7CF&scp=2&sq=Jeff+Davis+Coming+Around&st=p. *New York Times*. May 14, 1887. Retrieved 2011-06-10.
[10] Strode 1955, pp. 4-5.
[11] Strode 1955, pp. 11-27.
[12] Hamilton, Holman (1978). "Jefferson Davis Before His Presidency". *The Three Kentucky Presidents*. Lexington: University Press of Kentucky. ISBN 0813102464.
[13] U.S. Military Academy, Register of Officers and Graduates of the U.S. Military Academy from March 16, 1802 to January 1, 1850. Compiled by Capt. George W. Cullum. West Point, N.Y.: 1850, p. 148.
[14] Strode 1955, p. 76.
[15] Cooper 2000, pp. 64-72.
[16] Cooper 2000, pp. 75-79. Davis 1991, p. 89.
[17] Strode 1955, pp. 136-137.
[18] Cooper 2000, pp. 84-88, 98-100.
[19] Cooper 2000, pp. 90-115.
[20] Strode 1955, pp. 242, 268.
[21] Strode 1955, p. 273.
[22] "Margaret Howell Davis Hayes Chapter No. 2652" http://www.coloradoudc.org/. Colorado United Daughters of the Confederacy. Retrieved 2011-07-20.
[23] Strode 1964, p. 436.
[24] Cooper 2000, p. 480.
[25] Cooper 2000, p. 595.
[26] Strode 1964, pp. 527-528.
[27] Strode 1955, p. 157.
[28] Strode 1955, pp. 161-162.
[29] Strode 1955, pp. 164-167.
[30] Strode 1955, p. 188.
[31] Dodd 1907, pp. 12, 93.
[32] Strode 1955, p. 195.
[33] Rives, George Lockhart (1913). *The United States and Mexico, 1821-1848* http://books.google.com/books?id=vfhAAAAAIAAJ. New York: Charles Scribner's Sons. pp. 634-636.
[34] McPherson, James M. (1989). *Battle Cry of Freedom: The Civil War Era*. New York: Bantam Books. p. 104.
[35] Strode 1955, p. 210.

[36] $100,000 in 1849 would be worth more than $2,000,000 in 2010.Williamson, Samuel H. (2011). *Seven Ways to Compute the Relative Value of a U.S. Dollar Amount, 1774 to present.* MeasuringWorth http://www.measuringworth.com.
[37] Thomson, Janice E. (1996). *Mercenaries, Pirates and Sovereigns.* Princeton University Press. p. 121.
[38] Strode 1955, pp. 211-212.
[39] Rowland, Dunbar (1912). *The Official and Statistical Register of the State of Mississippi* http://books.google.com/books?id=-MoGAQAAIAAJ&pg=PA111&vq=foote&dq=henry+s+foote+1851&source=gbs_search_s&cad=0. Mississippi Department of Archives and History. Nashville, Tennessee: Press of Brandon Printing Company. p. 111. Retrieved 2009-03-26.
[40] Dodd 1907, pp. 130-131.
[41] Kleber, John E., ed (1992). "Davis, Jefferson". *The Kentucky Encyclopedia*. Associate editors: Thomas D. Clark, Lowell H. Harrison, and James C. Klotter. Lexington, Kentucky: The University Press of Kentucky. ISBN 0813117720.
[42] Dodd 1907, pp. 80, 133-135.
[43] Dodd 1907, pp. 152-153.
[44] Dodd 1907, pp. 12, 171-172.
[45] Cooper 2000, p. 3.
[46] "Jefferson Davis' Farewell" http://senate.gov/artandhistory/history/minute/Jefferson_Davis_Farewell.htm. United States Senate. Retrieved 2011-06-09.
[47] Cooper 2000, p. 322.
[48] Strode 1955, pp. 402-403.
[49] "Inaugural Address of President Davis" http://www.archive.org/stream/inauguraladdress00conf#page/n1/mode/2up. Montgomery, Alabama: Shorter and Reid, Printers. February 18, 1861. Retrieved 2011-07-17.
[50] Dodd 1907, pp. 197-198.
[51] "Jefferson Davis" http://www.civilwarhome.com/jdavisbio.htm. *Document.* www.civilwarhome.com.
[52] Cooper 2000, pp. 361-2.
[53] Cooper 2000, pp. 337-340.
[54] Strode 1959, pp. 90-94.
[55] Dodd 1907, p. 263.
[56] Dawson, Joseph G. III (April 2009). "Jefferson Davis and the Confederacy's "Offensive-Defensive" Strategy in the U.S. Civil War". *Journal of Military History* **73** (2): 591-607.
[57] Patrick 1944, pp. 49-50, 56.
[58] Patrick 1944, p. 51.
[59] Patrick 1944, p. 53.
[60] Patrick 1944, pp. 55-56.
[61] Patrick 1944, p. 57.
[62] Beringer, Richard E., Hattaway, Herman, Jones, Archer, and Still, William N., Jr. (1986). *Why the South Lost the Civil War*. Athens: University of Georgia Press.
[63] Woodworth, Steven E. (1990). *Jefferson Davis and His Generals: The Failure of Confederate Command in the West*. Lawrence: University Press of Kansas.
[64] Woodworth, Steven E. (1990). "Dismembering the Confederacy: Jefferson Davis and the Trans-Mississippi West". *Military History of the Southwest* **20** (1): 1-22.
[65] Hattaway and Beringer 2002.
[66] Escott 1978.
[67] Cooper 2000, pp. 475, 496.
[68] Andrews, J. Cutler (1966). "The Confederate Press and Public Morale". *Journal of Southern History* **32**.
[69] Cooper 2000, pp. 447, 480, 496.
[70] Cooper 2000, p. 511.
[71] Keegan, John (2009). *The American Civil War: A Military History*. Vintage Books. pp. 375-376. ISBN 978-0-307-27314-7.
[72] Dodd 1907, pp. 353-357.

[73] Winters, John D. (1963). *The Civil War in Louisiana*. Baton Rouge: Louisiana State University Press. p. 419. ISBN 0-8071-0834-0.

[74] "Jefferson Davis Was Captured" http://www.americaslibrary.gov/jb/civil/jb_civil_jeffdav_1.html. USA.gov. 2007. Retrieved 2010-02-04.

[75] "Capture of Jefferson Davis" http://www.georgiaencyclopedia.org/nge/Article.jsp?id=h-640. The New Georgia Encyclopedia. Retrieved 2011-06-08.

[76] Boone, Floyd E. (1988). *Florida Historical Markers & Sites: A Guide to More Than 700 Historic Sites*. Houston, Texas: Gulf Publishing Company. p. 15. ISBN 0-87201-558-0.

[77] "Historical Markers in Alachua County, Florida — DICKISON AND HIS MEN / JEFFERSON DAVIS' BAGGAGE" http://Growth-Management.Alachua.FL.US/historic/historic_commission/historical_markers/jeffdavistext.htm. Alachua County Historical Commission. Retrieved 2011-08-04.

[78] "Historic Markers Across Florida — Dickison and his men / Jefferson Davis' baggage" http://www.lat34north.com/HistoricMarkersFL/MarkerDetail.cfm?KeyID=001-1&MarkerTitle=Dickison%20and%20his%20men%20/%20Jefferson%20Davis%27%20baggage. Latitude 34 North. Retrieved 2011-08-04.

[79] Strode 1964, p. 302.

[80] Kevin Levin. "Update on Jefferson Davis's Crown of Thorns" http://cwmemory.com/2009/09/27/update-on-jefferson-daviss-crown-of-thorns/. Civil War Memory. Retrieved 2011-08-21.

[81] Strode 1964, pp. 402-404.

[82] Cooper 2000, pp. 574, 575, 602, 603.

[83] Strode 1964, pp. 439-441, 448-449.

[84] Cooper 2000, p. 658.

[85] Cooper 2000, pp. 652-654.

[86] Charles E. Fenner. "Eulogy of Robert E. Lee" http://leearchive.wlu.edu/reference/misc/fenner/index.html.

[87] Collins 2005.

[88] "Jefferson Finis Davis" http://www.findagrave.com/cgi-bin/fg.cgi?page=gr&GSln=davis&GSfn=Jefferson&GSmn=finis&GSbyrel=in&GSdyrel=in&GSob=n&GRid=260&. Find a Grave. 2001. Retrieved 2011-06-08.

[89] Urquhart, Kenneth Trist (March 21, 1959). "Seventy Years of the Louisiana Historical Association" http://www.lahistory.org/uploads/UrquhartLHAHistoryFinal.pdf (PDF). Alexandria, Louisiana: Louisiana Historical Association. Retrieved July 21, 2010.

[90] "Jefferson Davis State Historic Site" http://parks.ky.gov/findparks/histparks/jd/. Kentucky State Parks. Retrieved 2011-07-17.

[91] "Beauvoir - The Jefferson Davis Home and Presidential Library" http://www.beauvoir.org/. Mississippi Division, Sons of Confederate Veterans. Retrieved 2011-07-17.

[92] "The Papers of Jefferson Davis" http://jeffersondavis.rice.edu/. Rice University. Retrieved 2011-07-17.

[93] "The 2010 Florida Statutes (including Special Session A)" http://www.leg.state.fl.us/statutes/index.cfm?App_mode=Display_Statute&Search_String=&URL=0600-0699/0683/Sections/0683.01.html. The Florida Legislature. Retrieved 2011-07-25.

[94] "State Public Holidays" http://www.washingtondc.worldweb.com/TravelEssentials/PublicHolidays/. World Web Technologies, Inc.. Retrieved 2011-07-25.

[95] "Days of public rest, legal holidays, and half-holidays" http://www.legis.state.la.us/lss/lss.asp?doc=74097. The Louisiana State Legislature. Retrieved 2011-07-25.

[96] "Memorial Day History" http://www1.va.gov/opa/speceven/memday/history.asp. United States Department of Veterans Affairs. Retrieved 2011-07-25.

[97] "Official State of Alabama Calend" http://www.info.alabama.gov/calendar.aspx. Alabama State Government. Retrieved 2011-07-25.

[98] "Mississippi Code of 1972 — SEC. 3-3-7. Legal holiday." http://www.mscode.com/free/statutes/03/003/0007.htm. LawNetCom, Inc.. Retrieved 2011-07-25.

[99] "State holidays" http://www.tsl.state.tx.us/ref/abouttx/holidays.html. Texas State Library. Retrieved 2011-07-25.

[100] Weingroff, Richard F. (2011-04-07). "Jefferson Davis Memorial Highway" http://www.fhwa.dot.gov/infrastructure/jdavis.cfm. *Highway History http://www.fhwa.dot.gov/infrastructure/*

history.cfm. Federal Highway Administration, United States Department of Transportation. Retrieved 2011-09-29.
[101] McCaffrey, Scott (2011-09-28). "Road Renaming Proves Another Chance to Re-Fight the Civil War" http//www.sungazette.net. *Arlington Sun Gazette.* Springfield, Virginia: Sun Gazette Newspapers. Retrieved 2011-09-29.
[102] http://www.questia.com/PM.qst?a=o&d=106229784
[103] http://www.questia.com/PM.qst?a=o&d=14023352
[104] http://books.google.com/books?id=xtJ2AAAAMAAJ&printsec=frontcover&source=gbs_ge_summary_r&cad=0#v=onepage&q&f=false
[105] http://www.questia.com/PM.qst?a=o&d=29306356
[106] http://www.questia.com/PM.qst?a=o&d=10417084
[107] http://encyclopediavirginia.org/Davis_Jefferson_1808-1889
[108] http://www.virginia.org/Listings/HistoricSites/HollywoodCemetery/
[109] http://www.gutenberg.org/author/Davis+Jefferson
[110] http://bioguide.congress.gov/scripts/biodisplay.pl?index=D000113
[111] NIE
[112] Klein (1962), pp. 11.
[113] *Official Records,* Series II, Vol. 3, pp. 338-340, 812-13, Vol. 4, pp. 31-32, 48.
[114] "Memoirs, ch.21" http://www.sonofthesouth.net/union-generals/sherman/memoirs/general-sherman-march-sea.htm. William Tecumseh Sherman. Retrieved 2010-05-20.
[115] Encyclopedia Britannica
[116] New Georgia Encyclopedia
[117] http://bioguide.congress.gov
[118] http://bioguide.congress.gov/scripts/biodisplay.pl?index=C000548
[119] http://www.georgiaencyclopedia.org/nge/Article.jsp?id=h-615
[120] http://www.ustreas.gov/education/history/secretaries/hcobb.html
[121] http://www.findagrave.com/cgi-bin/fg.cgi?page=gr&GRid=8962
[122] http://milledgeville.galileo.usg.edu/milledgeville/view?docId=news/srw1868/srw1868-0178.xml&query=howell%20cobb&brand=milledgeville-brand
[123] James M. McPherson, *Battle Cry of Freedom* (New York: Ballantine Books, 1989), p. 74, gives his weight as 90 pounds.
[124] http://ourgeorgiahistory.com/ogh/Alexander_Stephens
[125] William Y. Thompson, *Robert Toombs of Georgia* (Baton Rouge: Louisiana State University Press, 1966, p. 13
[126] Young, Cathy, Behind the Jeffersonian Veneer http://reason.com/archives/2005/06/01/behind-the-jeffersonian-veneer, *Reason*
[127] Allan Nevins, *The Improvised War, 1861-1862* (New York: Charles Scribner's Sons, 1959), p. 73.
[128] Schott, Thomas E. (1988). *Alexander H. Stephens of Georgia.* pp. 357 ff..
[129] Hornsby, Sadie B. (August 4, 1938). *Born in Slavery: Slave Narratives from the Federal Writers' Project, 1936-1938* http://memory.loc.gov/cgi-bin/ampage?collId=mesn&fileName=041/mesn041.db&recNum=54&itemLink=D?mesnbib:2:./temp/~ammem_sRsD::. Interview with Georgia Baker. Library of Congress. p. 51. Retrieved February 15, 2011.
[130] http://books.google.com/books?id=w_gHAQAAIAAJ&printsec=frontcover#v=onepage&q=&f=false
[131] http://books.google.com/books?id=88AEAAAAYAAJ&printsec=frontcover#v=onepage&q=&f=false
[132] http://books.google.com/books?id=_sV3AAAAMAAJ&printsec=frontcover#v=onepage&q=&f=false
[133] http://books.google.com/books?id=RkBwAAAAMAAJ&printsec=frontcover#v=onepage&q=&f=false
[134] http://bioguide.congress.gov/scripts/biodisplay.pl?index=S000854
[135] http://blueandgraytrail.com/event/Alexander_Stephens
[136] http://www2.hsp.org/collections/manuscripts/s/Stephens0627.html
[137] http://portagepub.com/products/causouth/index.html
[138] http://teachingamericanhistory.org/library/index.asp?documentprint=76

[139] http://www.adena.com/adena/usa/cw/cw223.htm
[140] http://www.etymonline.com/cw/cornerstone.htm
[141] http://www.gastateparks.org/info/ahsteph/
[142] William Y. Thompson, *Robert Toombs of Georgia*, (Baton Rouge: Louisiana State University Press, 1966, Library of Congress No. 66-25722, p. 38)
[143] Thompson, p 58
[144] Thompson, p. 25
[145] http://opinionator.blogs.nytimes.com/2011/01/27/the-south-rises-again-and-again-and-again/#more-78437
[146] http://www.washingtonwilkes.org
[147] http://www.georgiaencyclopedia.org/nge/Article.jsp?id=h-799
[148] http://bioguide.congress.gov/scripts/biodisplay.pl?index=T000313
[149] http://portagepub.com/products/causouth/index.html
[150] http://www.gutenberg.org/etext/26069
[151] http://dlg.galileo.usg.edu/CollectionsA-Z/zlrt_information.html
[152] "Southeastern Shipbuilding" http://shipbuildinghistory.com/history/shipyards/4emergencylarge/wwtwo/southeastern.htm. shipbuildinghistory.com. Retrieved 2009-12-16.
[153] "Legendary Coins and Currency: Confederacy, 10 dollars, 1863" http://americanhistory.si.edu/coins/printable/coin.cfm?coincode=5_07. National Museum of American History. Retrieved 2011-08-11.
[154] http://www.nikolasschiller.com/blog/index.php/archives/2010/07/02/6574/
[155] http://bioguide.congress.gov/scripts/biodisplay.pl?index=H000988
[156] http://www.findagrave.com/cgi-bin/fg.cgi?page=gr&GRid=8321194
[157] http://bioguide.congress.gov
[158] Patrick 1944, p. 105.
[159] Patrick 1944, pp. 104, 106, 110.
[160] Patrick 1944, p. 116-117.
[161] "LeRoy Pope Walker" http://www.findagrave.com/cgi-bin/fg.cgi?page=gr&GRid=11101. Find a Grave. Retrieved 2008-08-10.
[162] http://www.csawardept.com/history/Cabinet/LPWalker/index.html
[163] "Genealogy of the Page Family in Virginia" by Richard Channing Moore Page
[164] Goldberg, David E. "George Wythe Randolph (1818-1867)." http://www.EncyclopediaVirginia.org/Randolph_George_Wythe_1818-1867, *Encyclopedia Virginia*, Ed. Brendan Wolfe. 6 Apr. 2011. Virginia Foundation for the Humanities, accessed 6 April 2011
[165] http://www.findagrave.com/cgi-bin/fg.cgi?page=gr&GRid=11056
[166] http://bioguide.congress.gov/scripts/biodisplay.pl?index=S000220
[167] http://www.findagrave.com/cgi-bin/fg.cgi?page=gr&GRid=6005865
[168] http://www.spartacus.schoolnet.co.uk/USACWsneddon.htm
[169] http://www.csawardept.com/history/Cabinet/Seddon/index.html
[170] Woodworth, p. 360, n. 192.
[171] "John C. Breckinridge" http://www.doctorzebra.com/prez/a_breck.htm (Editorial). *New York Times*. 1863-12-07. Retrieved 2008-02-17.
[172] Hiking Colorado: An Atlas of Colorado's Greatest Hiking Adventures http//books.google.com, by Maryann Gaug, 2003, page 111
[173] Exploring Colorado Highways: Trip Trivia http//books.google.com, by Michael Heim, 2007, page 86
[174] Seven Perfect Days in Colorado: A Guided Driving Tour http//books.google.com, by Bill Ginnodo and Celia Ginnodo, 2007, page 45
[175] Newspaper article, Breckenridge or Breckinridge: Local Historian Breaks it Down http://www.vaildaily.com/article/20090613/NEWS/906139991/1062, by Robert Allen, Vail (Colorado) Daily, June 13, 2009
[176] http://bioguide.congress.gov/scripts/biodisplay.pl?index=B000789
[177] http://www.doctorzebra.com/prez/a_breck.htm
[178] http://www.archive.org/details/biographicalsket00demorich
[179] http://www.findagrave.com/cgi-bin/fg.cgi?page=gr&GRid=132

[180] Patrick 1944, p. 205.
[181] "Memminger, Charles Gustavus". *Appletons' Cyclopædia of American Biography*. 1900.
[182] "Memminger, Christopher Gustavus". *New International Encyclopedia*. 1905.
[183] Patrick 1944, pp. 205-206.
[184] "Memminger, Christopher Gustavus". *Encyclopedia Americana*. 1920.
[185] "Legendary Coins and Currency: Confederacy, 5 dollars, 1862" http://americanhistory.si.edu/coins/printable/coin.cfm?coincode=5_05. National Museum of American History. Retrieved 2011-08-12.
[186] Patrick 1944, pp. 236-237.
[187] Patrick 1944, pp. 237-238.
[188] Patrick 1944, p. 242.
[189] Allen, Felicity (1999), *Jefferson Davis, Unconquerable Heart* http://books.google.com/?id=56R_N48VhnkC (illustrated ed.), University of Missouri, p. 6, ISBN 0826212190, , retrieved 2009-03-03
[190] "Judah Philip Benjamin" http://www.answers.com/topic/judah-p-benjamin, *West's Encyclopedia of American Law*, accessed 21 July 2011
[191] Mosaic: Jewish Life in Florida (Coral Gables, FL: MOSAIC, Inc., 1991): 9
[192] "Review: 'Harby's Discourse on the Jewish Synagogue, and the Constitution of the Reform Congregation'". *The North American Review* **23** (52): 67-79. 1826. JSTOR 25102552.
[193] de Ville, Winston (1996). "The Marriage Contract of Judah P. Benjamin and Natalie St. Martin". *Louisiana History* **37** (1): 81-84. JSTOR 4233263.
[194] Lebeson, Anita Libman (1975). *Pilgrim People: A History of the Jews in America from 1492 to 1974*. New York: Minerva Press. p. 27. ISBN 0308101561.
[195] Carl Sandburg, *Abraham Lincoln The Prairie Years and the War Years*, NY, Harcourt Brace and Co., 1956, p. 239
[196] "Judah P. Benjamin" http://www.civilwarhome.com/benjaminbio.htm, excerpted from Eli N. Evans, "The Confederacy," *MacMillan Information Now Encyclopedia*, at Home of the American Civil War website, accessed 24 July 2011. (Note: Evans is a contemporary biographer of Benjamin. A superior source is required, as similar quotes are often attributed to UK Prime Minister Benjamin Disraeli).
[197] "The Brains of the Confederacy" http://www.jewish-history.com/civilwar/judahpb.html, excerpted from Herbert T. Ezekiel and Gaston Lichtenstein, *The History of the Jews of Richmond from 1769 to 1917*, Richmond: H. T. Ezekiel, Printer and Publisher, 1917, p. 166; as *Jews in the Civil War*, Jewish-American History Foundation, Retrieved November 21, 2008
[198] John D. Winters, *The Civil War in Louisiana*, Baton Rouge: Louisiana State University Press, 1963, ISBN 0-8071-0834-0, pp. 72, 78
[199] "Judah P. Benjamin" http://www.answers.com/topic/judah-p-benjamin#ixzz1T26i8OhB, *Oxford Dictionary of the US Military*, at Answers.com, accessed 24 July 2011
[200] "Judah P. Benjamin" http://www.answers.com/topic/judah-p-benjamin#ixzz1T26i8OhB, *Gale Encyclopedia of Biography*, at Answers.com, accessed 24 July 2011
[201] "Wilkes County, Georgia - The Story of Washington-Wilkes part V" http://www.giddeon.com/wilkes/history/soww5.shtml. Giddeon.com. Retrieved 2010-01-31.
[202] Ott, Eloise Robinson, and Chazal, Louis Hickman, *Ocali Country*, Ocala: Marion Publishers, 1966, p. 87
[203] "Florida State Parks - Judah P. Benjamin Confederate Memorial at (Gamble Plantation) State Historic Site" http://www.abfla.com/parks/GamblePlantation/gambleplantation.html. Abfla.com. Retrieved 2010-01-31.
[204] Lebeson, *Pilgrim People*, 1975, p. 275
[205] *American History*, Volume 40, Issues 1-6. Cowles History Group, a division of Cowles Magazines, 2005. p. 63
[206] Simmons, Donald C. (2001). *Confederate Settlements in British Honduras*. Jefferson, NC: McFarland. ISBN 0786410167.
[207] http//books.google.com
[208] http://www.nytimes.com/2010/01/01/arts/design/01antiques.html
[209] http://books.google.com/books?id=Tkg8AAAAIAAJ&q=Korn
[210] http://bioguide.congress.gov/scripts/biodisplay.pl?index=B000365

[211] http://www.jewishvirtuallibrary.org/jsource/biography/Benjamin.html
[212] http://photos.historical-markers.org/v/northcarolina/nc-newhanover/006_0332.JPG.html
[213] http://docsouth.unc.edu/nc/demconserv/demconserv.html
[214] "Thomas Bragg" http://www.findagrave.com/cgi-bin/fg.cgi?page=gr&GRid=7147679. Find a Grave. Retrieved 2011-08-13.
[215] Thomas Bragg http://bioguide.congress.gov/scripts/biodisplay.pl?index=B000759 at the *Biographical Directory of the United States Congress*
[216] "Liberty Ships - Part 2: EMC #s 768 thru 1551" http://shipbuildinghistory.com/history/merchantships/wwii/libertyships2.htm. shipbuildinghistory.com. Retrieved 2011-08-13.
[217] http://www.findagrave.com/cgi-bin/fg.cgi?page=gr&GRid=8065987
[218] http://www.csawardept.com/history/Cabinet/GDavis/
[219] "REAGAN, John Henninger, (1818 - 1905) " http://bioguide.congress.gov/scripts/biodisplay.pl?index=r000098. Biographical Directory of the United States Congress. Retrieved 27 November 2010.
[220] "REAGAN, JOHN HENNINGER " http://www.tshaonline.org/handbook/online/articles/fre02. Texas State Historical Association. Retrieved 27 November 2010.
[221] "John Henninger Reagan (2) " http://www.txgenweb5.org/txkaufman/wall/reaganjh.htm. Kaufman County TXGenWeb Project. Retrieved 27 November 2010.
[222] Raines, Cadwell Walton (1902). *Year book for Texas*. Gammel Book Company.
[223] Boyd B. Stutler, 1962. "The Confederate Postal Service in West Virginia" http://www.wvculture.org/history/journal_wvh/wvh24-1.html. West Virginia Archives and History . . Retrieved 19 November 2010.
[224] Find a Grave http://www.findagrave.com/cgi-bin/fg.cgi?page=gr&GRid=6221943
[225] http://texashistory.unt.edu/permalink/meta-pth-39141:1
[226] http://bioguide.congress.gov/scripts/biodisplay.pl?index=R000098
[227] http://www.tshaonline.org/handbook/online/articles/RR/fre2.html
[228] http://www.findagrave.com/cgi-bin/fg.cgi?page=gr&GRid=6221943
[229] http://www.smokykin.com/tng/getperson.php?personID=I723&tree=Smokykin
[230] Scharf, *Confederate States Navy*, p. 29n, states that he was born in 1813. Durkin, *Confederate Navy Chief*, p. 11n, asserts that Mallory in his childhood diary wrote that his age was nine when he began school in 1820. Most historians favor the later date, but they acknowledge that records are lacking. Mallory's tombstone in St. Michael's Cemetery, Pensacola, Florida, gives the year of 1812, but no exact birthdate:http://www.findagrave.com/cgi-bin/fg.cgi?page=pv&GRid=21357&PIpi=6333388.
[231] Some historians (Durkin, Luraghi, Wise) write that the father's given name was John, others (Scharf, Underwood) that it was Charles. Underwood, *Mallory*, p. 6, has the support of a family tradition.
[232] Luraghi, *Confederate States Navy*, p. 10.
[233] Durkin, *Confederate Navy Chief*, pp. 14-15.
[234] Luraghi, *Confederate Navy*, pp. 10-11. In the absence of law schools, "reading law" under the tutelage of a practicing member was the customary method of preparing for entry into the profession.
[235] Durkin, *Confederate Navy Chief*, pp. 31-32.
[236] Underwood, *Mallory*, p. 187.
[237] Clubbs, Florida Historical Quarterly, vol. 25, no. 3, pp. 232, 235, 236-237, 240. While serving as judge, the name of the court was changed to Probate Court.
[238] Durkin, *Confederate Navy Chief*, pp. 38-39.
[239] Underwood, *Mallory*, p. 21.
[240] Durkin, *Confederate Navy Chief*, p. 38-43, 48-49.
[241] Underwood, *Mallory*, pp. 22-25.
[242] Durkin, *Confederate Navy Chief*, pp. 56-60.
[243] His other initial committee assignment was to the minor Committee on Engrossed Bills. *Congressional Globe*, 32nd Congress, 1st session, p. 32.
[244] *Congressional Globe*, 32nd Congress, 1st session, p. 19.
[245] Durkin, *Confederate Navy Chief*, pp. 52-55.

[246] Mallory's remarks can be read in full: *Congressional Globe,* 32nd Congress, 1st session, Appendix, pp. 108-119.
[247] After 1853. Underwood, *Mallory,* p. 29.
[248] Durkin, *Confederate Navy Chief,* pp. 70-83.
[249] Tucker, *Naval Warfare,* pp. 51-57, 62. One of the first class of frigates, USS *Merrimack,* would later become more closely identified with Mallory's vision of the maritime future.
[250] Durkin, *Confederate Navy Chief,* pp. 63-64.
[251] Durkin, *Confederate Navy Chief,* p. 101. Similarly Underwood, *Mallory,* p. 38. His speech cannot be termed an oration. Although the language was sometimes floral in the manner of the time, his voice was so low that at one point he had to be interrupted by a request that he speak louder.
[252] *Congressional Globe,* 35th Congress, 1st session, p. 1136-1140 (March 16, 1858). Mallory's revised remarks also can be found in *Congressional Globe,* 35th Congress, 1st session, Appendix, pp. 214-218.
[253] Underwood, *Mallory,* pp. 70-71. See *Congressional Globe,* 36th Congress, 2nd session, pp. 485-486.
[254] Underwood, *Mallory,* p. 67. Two other forts near Pensacola, Forts Barrancas and McRee, were occupied by Florida militia without incident.
[255] Underwood, *Mallory,* pp. 68-70-73.
[256] Durkin, *Confederate Navy Chief,* pp. 132-133.
[257] "Cabinet, Confederate States," in Faust, *Encyclopedia.* The only other cabinet nomination to draw as much opposition was that of Judah P. Benjamin.
[258] Underwood, *Mallory,* pp. 77-79.
[259] Underwood, *Mallory,* pp. 86-87.
[260] Luraghi, *Confederate Navy,* pp. 35-36.
[261] Underwood, *Mallory,* p. 87. The Torpedo Bureau was headed initially by Mallory's antagonist Matthew F. Maury.
[262] Durkin, *Confederate Navy Chief,* p. 148.
[263] Durkin, *Confederate Navy Chief,* p. 284.
[264] Underwood, *Mallory,* p. 169.
[265] Durkin, *Confederate Navy Chief,* pp. 158-160.
[266] Anderson, *By Sea and by River,* p. 44.
[267] The raiders can be counted on one's fingers: *Sumter, Alabama, Georgia, Florida, Shenandoah, Nashville.*
[268] Tucker, *Naval Warfare,*, p. 110.
[269] Underwood, *Mallory,* p. 114.
[270] Anderson, *By Sea and by River,* pp. 212-214.
[271] ORN, ser. II, vol. 2, p. 51. Mallory, Report of the Secretary of the Navy to the President, April 26, 1861. Note that his ideal warship, combining speed, firepower, and armor, was not achieved until the 1930s, at the end of the battleship era. Tucker, *Naval Warfare,* p. 226.
[272] Luraghi, *Confederate Navy,* pp. 68, 89-90.
[273] The first Confederate ironclad, CSS *Manassas,* was converted by private parties who intended to use her as a privateer.
[274] Underwood, *Mallory,* p. 99.
[275] Simson, *Naval Strategies,* p. 60.
[276] Hearn, *Capture of New Orleans,* pp. 143-147.
[277] Underwood, *Mallory,* p. 83.
[278] Luraghi, *Confederate Navy,* pp. 91-92.
[279] Luraghi, *Confederate Navy,* pp.217-233.
[280] With little evidence in support, naval theorists in the mid-nineteenth century thought that the primary weapon of armored ships should be a reinforced bow that would enable them to destroy enemy ships by ramming. Ram bows became a standard feature of warships built almost to the start of World War I, although improved gunnery had made them anachronistic almost from the start. Even CSS *Virginia* was often referred to as a ram, as if that were her most significant feature. Tucker, *Naval Warfare.* pp. 97, 132-133.
[281] Luraghi, *Confederate Navy,* pp. 265-271.

[282] The cover of Underwood's biography of the man shows his portrait against the backdrop of the battle between the ironclads *Monitor* and *Virginia* - or, as it was known even in the Confederacy, as the Battle between the *Monitor* and *Merrimack*.
[283] Underwood, *Mallory*, p. 139.
[284] Underwood, *Mallory*, p. 149. The Torpedo Bureau, with which the Service cooperated, was run by the War Department.
[285] Luraghi, *Confederate Navy*, p. 247.
[286] Tucker, *Naval Warfare*, pp. 167-168.
[287] Durkin, *Confederate Navy Chief*, p. 264.
[288] G. J. Rains, "Torpedoes," Southern Historical Society Papers, v. III, p. 256 (1877).
[289] Underwood, *Mallory*, p. 153.
[290] Most accounts of the *Hunley-Housatonic* encounter fail to mention that the former was actually traveling on the surface at the time of the attack. See Tucker, *Naval Warfare*, pp. 177-178.
[291] Underwood, *Mallory*, p. 164.
[292] Underwood, *Mallory*, pp. 111-112.
[293] Underwood, *Mallory*, pp. 174-178.
[294] Underwood, *Mallory*, pp. 178-179.
[295] Underwood, *Mallory*, pp. 179-184.
[296] Underwood, *Mallory*, pp. 203-204.
[297] Underwood, *Mallory*, pp. 207-208.
[298] Underwood, *Mallory*, p. 210.
[299] http://bioguide.congress.gov/scripts/biodisplay.pl?index=M000084

Article Sources and Contributors

The sources listed for each article provide more detailed licensing information including the copyright status, the copyright owner, and the license conditions.

Jefferson Davis *Source:* http://en.wikipedia.org/w/index.php?oldid=457831032 *License:* Creative Commons Attribution-Share Alike 3.0 Unported *Contributors:* 1337 sp43k l0l, 17Spartacus76, 21655, 28421u2232nfenfcenc, 777sms, 8th Ohio Volunteers, A. B., Abel moreno, Absecon 59, Academic Challenger, Access Denied, Acctorp, Acdixon, Acp 1987, Adder7289, Addihockey10, Addshore, Agüeybaná, Ahoerstemeier, AidanPalmer, Aitias, Alansohn, Alex.muller, Alex2706, Alfirin, AlleywayRover, Allstarecho, Alodyne, AlphaEta, Amatulic, Amcbride, AmericanCentury21, Amplitude101, Andy Marchbanks, AndyTheGrump, Antandrus, Antipatros, Appalachianangler, Aquillion, Argyll Lassie, Ari Publican, Ark30inf, ArmadilloFromHell, Arniep, Asbel, Astrangemeaning, Astynax, Auburnfan29, Aude, Avazina, Awsomewindow, AzaToth, B, BCV, Baa, Baboo, Badbilltucker, Barliner, Barneyboo, Bbflik, Beck, Bedford, Ben76266, Bencherlite, Berean Hunter, Bettymnz4, Bewildebeast, Bigfatblackbelt, Bigfrie192, Bill Thayer, Billinghurst, Billwhittaker, Billy Hathorn, BillyPreset, Biruitorul, Bjoel5785, Bkonrad, Bkwillwm, BlacksheepPAUL, Blinking Spirit, BlueMoonlet, Bluemoose, BobTheTomato, Bobianite, Bobo192, Boccobrock, Bonadea, Bongwarrior, BorgQueen, Bradus, Brandon5485, Brian Joseph Morgan, BrtnMonster, Bruce1ee, Bruske, Bsadowski1, Bthayesesq, Bubba73, BuddyxXx, Bujbrother, Bullytr, BusterD, Buxtehude76, CJHaynes, CORNELIUSSEON, Calmer Waters, Calstanhope, Caltas, CambridgeBayWeather, Cameron12355, Cameronprine, Can't sleep, clown will eat me, Can'tStandYa, CanadianLinuxUser, Canderson7, Canis Lupus, CantStandYa, Canuckian89, Caponer, Capt Jim, Carlaude, Catwhoorg, CelticJobber, Centpacrr, Chachap, Chairboy, Chanceinator, Charles Matthews, Charles Nguyen, Chenhsi, Chiefsalsa, Chris the speller, Christian Historybuff, Chuck369, Chuckiesdad, Civil Engineer III, Claffey27, Cleared as filed, Cmguy777, Coingeek, Colincbn, Cometstyles, CommonsDelinker, Complex01, Connormah, ConspiraFear, Conversion script, Cooatridge, Corker1, CountingPine, Courcelles, Crazy Boris with a red beard, Crazycomputers, Crazyfurf, Cricketgirl, CryptoDerk, Cuchullain, Cun, Curtis23, CutOffTies, CyberRaptor, D-Rock, D6, DARTH SIDIOUS 2, DCEdwards1966, DMG413, DNewhall, DVD R W, Daffy123, Dangerousjimmycanada, DanielDeibler, DarkAudit, Darth Kalwejt, Davehi1, Davepape, David Haslam, DavidA, Dchall1, Ddye, De Administrando Imperio, Delirium, DeltaQuad, Den fjättrade ankan, DerHexer, Derumi, DevastatorIIC, Dezidor, Dferg47, Dfrg.msc, Dger, Digitalme, Dionyseus, Discospinster, Dismas, Dk1965, Docu, Document, Don4of4, Doug Coldwell, Doulos Christos, Download, Dr. Sunglasses, DrFrench, Drestros power, Driam, Drmies, Dsmdgold, Dspradau, Dukeruckley, Dunee, Durova, Duroy, DutchmanInDisguise, Dvmlny, Dysepsion, ESkog, ESpublic013, Edward, El aprendelenguas, ElTyrant, Elenseel, Emote, Enh4nc3d5p4rk, Enosfam, Enviroboy, Enyavar, Epachamo, Epbr123, Ericamick, Ericl, Ericl234, Esemono, Ettenro, Evan McMullen, Everyguy, Everyking, Ewulp, Exert, Eyal Bairey, Ezratrumpet, F2fox04, FHSerkland, Fan-1967, Fattyjwoods, Fcd345, FeanorStar7, Fieldday-sunday, Figma, Fingers-of-Pyrex, Flexiblefine, Floydspinky71, Flyguy649, Foochar, Foofbun, Formulax, Foxyshadis, Frank, FrankCostanza, Freakmighty, Freakofnurture, FredR, Freedomlinux, Freedotift, Funnyfarmofdoom, Furrykef, G.-M. Cupertino, Gaius Cornelius, Galoubet, GeneralPatton, Geodyde, Gidonb, Gil Gamesh, Gilliam, Gimboid13, Glacier Wolf, Goatasaur, Goblinpwn1, Golbez, Good Olfactory, GoodDay, Goustien, GrandWizard, Greatestrowerever, Greg jinkerson, Greyfox-csa, Griffinity, GrooveDog, Grubbmeister, Gscshoyru, Gsmgm, Guanaco, Gundersen53, Gunnernett, Gurch, Gurchzilla, Gwillhickers, Habap, HailFire, HalfShadow, HamburgerRadio, HanzoHattori, HarlandQPitt, Hasotweb, Haukurth, Hcballer257, Helth, Hephaestos, Hiddekel, Hlj, Hmains, Holtyw!, Homagetocatalonia, Hopeknowsall, Hoponpop69, Hq3473, Hvn0413, Hydriotaphia, IRP, IRelayer, IW.HG, Ian Rose, Imaninjapirate, Immortal Glory, Infrogmation, Insanityluffer, Intelati, Iridescent, IronDuke, Irregulargalaxies, Isfisk, Isis, Ivan1984, Ixfd64, J.delanoy, JForget, JHMM13, JLaTondre, JNW, JW1805, JWB, Jack Bethune, Jack O'Lantern, Jackfork, Jake Wartenberg, James.bulfinch, JamesBWatson, Jameshardy01, Jamie@jamiejamie.com, Jancarhart, Jaranda, Java13690, Jay Litman, JayJasper, Jayron32, Jclemens, Jcounterman98, JediSnoopy, Jef-Infojef, Jehorn, Jengod, Jersey emt, Jhinman, JimVC3, JimWae, Jkelly, Jklin, Jll, Jmlk17, Jni, JoanneB, JodyB, Joe mog, Joewithajay, John K, John Lake, John Mehlberg, John of Reading, Jojhutton, Jonathunder, Jonnysplatz, JordeeBec, Jordon Kalilich, Joseph Solis in Australia, Josephabradshaw, Joshmaul, Joyous!, Jtir, Jtjn6, Jua Cha, JuicyVuittionCouture, Juliancolton, Just H, JustAGal, Justanyone, Jwillbur, KAVEBEAR, KJS77, Ka Faraq Gatri, Kaaveh Ahangar, Kanags, Katalaveno, Katieh5584, Kbdank71, Keegan, Keilana, Ken Gallager, Kentworth, Khan singh, Kingpin13, Kingturtle, Kinneyboy90, Kiteinthewind, Kjetil r, KnowledgeOfSelf, Kresock, KuatofKDY, Kumioko, Kusma, Kyorosuke, LB-Versender, Lakers, LarryJeff, Lebezki, Ledzeppelin321295, LegendLiver, Leuko, LevelCheck, Levineps, Lewisskinner, LibLord, Lightmouse, Lihaas, Lima bean of the north, Lipsio, Lockesdonkey, Logicalleft, Looper5920, Loren.wilton, Losergeekneil, Luna Santin, M, MONGO, MPS, MPerel, Macleodloud, Madhero88, Magnus Manske, Mandarax, MarcusVenator, Marek69, Margo&Gladys, Mark K. Jensen, MarkSweep, Markduanewilliams, Marketinggal, Marktreut, MarmadukePercy, MartinezMD, Mausy5043, Mav, Mayumashu, Mbj360, Mbourgon, Meelar, Melsaran, MemoryHole.com, Mentifisto, Mercury, Mfields1, Micagi, Michael Hardy, MichaelBillington, Michaelas10, Mifter, Mike Rosoft, Mike hayes, Mikeblas, Miller17CU94, Mimithebrain, Mindmatrix, Minimac's Clone, Mithras6, Mkamensek, Modernist, Monegasque, Monsieurtode, Monterey Bay, Monty845, Mr Stephen, MrDolomite, MrFish, MrPrada, Mrbobmac, Mrdie, Mschel, Mschlindwein, Muboshgu, Mutinus, My name, Myanw, Mykej, N5iln, Nakon, Nat Krause, Natalie Erin, Nathan000000, Nathanholder, Nathanpadams2, Natural Cut, Naughty.frog, NawlinWiki, NekoDaemon, NellieBly, Nengscoz416, Neutrality, Nevilley, NewEnglandYankee, Newone, Nick Number, Nickels89, Nishkid64, Niteowlneils, Nitsirt, Nk, Nlu, No Guru, Noah Salzman, Nono64, North Shoreman, Nsamuels, Nymf, Octane, OhanaUnited, Oldlaptop321, Oli Filth, Omicronpersei8, Omnedon, Oren neu dag, Owned14, Oxymoron83, PJM, PTSE, Packerfansam, Parkwells, PatBethea, Patriciaharrod, Patrickneil, Peanutmojam, PearlWashington, Pearle, Pechmerle, PedanticallySpeaking, Pepper, Persian Poet Gal, Peruvianllama, PeterSymonds, Pgk, Philip Stevens, Phonecloth 554, Pibwl, Pilotguy, Pizza1512, Plau, Poindexter Propellerhead, Pokemonstinksalot, Politicaljunkie23, Porcupinefish, Postdlf, Prayerfortheworld, President Rhapsody, Promethean, PrometheusX303, Prunedaler, Pteron, Public Kanonkas, Puchiko, Pufferfish101, Qtoktok, QueenCake, Quendus, Quintote, Qxz, RFD, RPellessier, RSStockdale, RWReagan, Radon210, Random User 937494, Raphael123456789, Raven4x4x, Rbehrns, Redbar0nz, Redfarmer, Redrocket, Remember, RexNL, Rhobite, RicHard-59, Rich Farmbrough, Richard75, RickK, Rillian, Rito Revolto, Rjensen, Rjwilmsi, Roadrunner, Robert K S, Robert1947, Rocketbatter, RodC, Romanm, Roscocarter, Rpeh, Rtb2425, Rubbrchikin, Rupertslander, RxS, Ryan Vesey, Ryantang20, S3000, SGT141, SHLAMA, STHayden, Safety Cap, Saforrest, Sahasrahla, Sango123, Sarsaparilla, Saunderz911, Savh, Saxifrage, Saxonjf, Saywhaaa, Scarian, Scewing, Schmendrick, Scientizzle, Scott Burley, Scott Mingus, Sean William, Seaphoto, Searcher 1990, Secret Saturdays, Seminole Sam, Senatus, Settler, Shanem201, Sharkface217, Shell Kinney, Sherurcij, Short Angle, Show0591, SidP, Sidesthat thats hn, Sidioustyranus02, Simoncursitor, Sir Intellegence, SirAndrew1, Sjakkalle, Skamite, Skate12, Skeejay, Skenmy, SkerHawx, Skoolkid1, Skylerevans, Slipperyweasel, Slkirmes, Smack, SmartGuy, Smoove Z, Sniffersnify, Snowolf, SoWhy, Soccerguy97, Soccerluke22, Solarusdude, Soldan, Some jerk on the Internet, Son, Sonicspike, Sonpraises, Spadetalk, Speedoflight, Speedracer531, Spitfire, SpookyMulder, Stan Shebs, StaticGull, Staticshakedown, Steezmaster, StephenBuxton, Steve Casburn, Steven J. Anderson, Steven Zhang, Sturm55, SudoGhost, Suffusion of Yellow, Suimpos, Supergodzilla2090, Swedhombre, Swimmingmadcow, Swvalaw, Tad Lincoln, Tagishsimon, Takethemud, Taneya, Tanthalas39, Tassedethe, Tbhotch, TedE, Tedickey, Tellyaddict, Terryn3, Tevyus, Texas.veggie, TexasAndroid, Thaurisil, The Hybrid, The Mystery Man, The Rambling Man, The Thing That Should Not Be, The Tramp, The Utahraptor, The juggresurection, The stuart, TheChimp, TheDJ, TheMoot, Thechanger25998, Thehelpfulone, Theleftorium, Themunchkineer, Thesouthernhistorian45, Thingg, Thismightbezach, Tiddly Tom, Tide rolls, Tim Cox, Tim1965, TimMagic, Timber94, Tktru, Tkundercover, Tniem, Tom, Tom-, TommyBoy, Tovojolo, Tpbradbury, TransUtopian, Treybien, Trusilver, Twintone, Unibod, Unschool, Unyoyega, Urbanrenewal, User2004, Vanished user 39948282, Vaoverland, Vary, Velella, Venske, Ventusa, Verrai, Versageek, Versus22, Viriditas, Vital Component, VolatileChemical, Voldemore, Voyagerfan5761, Vrenator, Vzbs34, Wackowarrior, Wallie, Waterferder, Wayne Slam, WehrWolf, Wenli, Weyes, Whatusernameisnttaken, Wheasley, WhisperToMe, White Shadows, Whomp, Whosyourjudas, WiccaIrish, WikiLaurent, Wikid77, Wikidudeman, Wikieditor1553, Wikipelli, Will Beback, WillC, Willking1979, Wimt, Wknight94, Wmahan, Wokkadee, Womble, Woohookitty, Wooyi, Writtenright, Wwoods, Wyldephang, Wyss, XQ fan, XR-23, Xaosflux, Xasz, Xeroith, Xtreambar, Yamamoto Ichiro, YanA, Yancyfry jr, Ylee, Yomomma23234, Yongbyong38, Youfamissim, Yuirwood, ZEM1272, Zainaldin, Zantastik, Zeamays, Zhudyzhu, Zoe, ZooFari, 1831 anonymous edits 3

Howell Cobb *Source:* http://en.wikipedia.org/w/index.php?oldid=448549674 *License:* Creative Commons Attribution-Share Alike 3.0 Unported *Contributors:* Antodav2007, Ari Publican, BD2412, Bbsrock, Catapult, Complex01, Connormah, D6, DLJessup, Danheac, Darth Kalwejt, Donrell, Epolk, Ericl, Ettrig, FHSerkland, Fat pig73, FourthAve, GhostofSuperslum, Good Olfactory, GoodDay, HennessyC, Hlj, Hmains, Hydriotaphia, Inwind, JForget, JW1805, Jack Cox, Jengod, Jjmillerhistorian, John K, Kchishol1970, Khatru2, Koavf, Kumioko, Legalbeagle10, Monegasque, NawlinWiki, Neutrality, Newyorkbrad, Nkrosse, North Shoreman, Packerfansam, PaulinSaudi, Peter200, RFD, RWReagan, Ravenswing, Richard75, Roswell native, RustySpear, Sardanaphalus, Scott Mingus, Snowolf, SoundGod3, Steve Casburn, TJRC, The Mystery Man, Thismightbezach, Tom, Twinsrulemlb, Valadius, Verne Equinox, W Webb Research, W guice, WOSlinker, Александр Мотин, 35 anonymous edits 25

Alexander H. Stephens *Source:* http://en.wikipedia.org/w/index.php?oldid=446164718 *License:* Creative Commons Attribution-Share Alike 3.0 Unported *Contributors:* 2fort5r, ATL-Rob, Abrech, Adamlazzara, Alansohn, AmbassadorShras, Antipatros, Appraiser, Astynax, BCV, Baysage, Bbsrock, Ben76266, Benjiboi, Billy Hathorn, Biruitorul, Bogey97, BoiGayzer, BusterD, CIreland, CambridgeBayWeather, Caspian blue, Catapult, Celarnor, Chuunen Baka, Como, Connormah, Corpx, D6, Darkfight, Darolew, Darth Kalwejt, Darwinek, Davemck, Davemcle, Dawginroswell, DerHexer, Discospinster, Dudeman5685, Edward, Eliyak, Emoscopes, Emote, Evlekis, Ewlyahoocom, Ezratrumpet, Feedmecereal, Fish Cop, Fogster, Frosted14, GcSwRhIc, General Eisenhower, Good Olfactory, GoodDay, Grey Knight 1ce, Griot, Haham hanuka, Hephaestos, Hmains, I am you dad, Infrogmation, Inwind, IronDuke, JLaTondre, Jack Cox, JamesMLane, Jengod, Jim.henderson, Jmlk17, JoJo Galvez, John K, Johnny cash1, Jojhutton, Jolomo, Josephabradshaw, Kendrick7, Khassani, Kid Hum, Kingturtle, Koavf, Kresock, KuatofKDY, Kumioko, LB-Versender, Levelistchampion, Little Savage, Magnus Manske, Marek69, Mark K. Jensen, Matt Britt, MattSal, MaxVeers, Mboverload, Mbr7975, Mdotley, Melesse, Mm6119, Monacat, Monegasque, NapoleonX, Niteowlneils, North Shoreman, Onorem, Otolemur crassicaudatus, PJtP, ParisianBlade, Pecka92, Philip Stevens, Phoe, Powerknit, Psycho Kirby, Qqqqqq, RPH, Ramorum, Rich Farmbrough, RickK, Rjensen, Roswell native, Rrostrom, Saffi2k7, Sardanaphalus, Schafesd, SchuminWeb, Sciurinæ, Scott Mingus, Seattledude, Settler, Shsilver, SpeDIt, TJRC, TOO, TexasAndroid, ThJefferson, That-Vela-Fella, The Mystery Man, TheParanoidOne, Thismightbezach, Tom, Tomas417,

Tpbradbury, TransUtopian, Treybien, VastTriumph, Walden69, Warpflyght, WillC, Woohookitty, XR-23, Y, Zachary Klaas, Æthelwold, 154 anonymous edits ... 33

Robert Toombs *Source:* http://en.wikipedia.org/w/index.php?oldid=443886760 *License:* Creative Commons Attribution-Share Alike 3.0 Unported *Contributors:* Acather96, Bbmap, Bearcat, Bigturtle, Billy Hathorn, Bobo192, Catapult, CleveHist, Complex01, D6, Damirgraffiti, Danny, Darwinek, Davepape, Donrell, Emote, Fransverhagen, Frietjes, Gaius Cornelius, Geogre, Good Olfactory, Grendelkhan, Hey Teacher, Hlj, Hmains, Jengod, Jmlk17, Joelfurr, Johnny cash1, Jojhutton, Khan singh, Khatru2, Km17, KuatofKDY, KudzuVine, Kumioko, LB-Versender, Lachaume, Minesweeper, Mpbndc, NawlinWiki, North Shoreman, Olivier, Packerfansam, PhilKnight, Postdlf, Rjensen, Roswell native, Rrius, Ruzulo, Scott Mingus, Ser Amantio di Nicolao, Smelialichu, Some jerk on the Internet, SpeDIt, Template namespace initialisation script, The Mystery Man, The Special Education Squad, Thismightbezach, Tktru, Tlmclain, Tom, Tomas417, Topbanana, Unyoyega, Walden69, Wknight94, 34 anonymous edits ... 43

Robert M. T. Hunter *Source:* http://en.wikipedia.org/w/index.php?oldid=449398923 *License:* Creative Commons Attribution-Share Alike 3.0 Unported *Contributors:* AP1787, AdamBMorgan, Americus55, BD2412, Bazj, Biruitorul, Brother Officer, Canuckian89, Catapult, Chris the speller, Complex01, Connormah, DLJessup, DavidWBrooks, Dimadick, Finley, GoldRingChip, Good Olfactory, Hmains, Iridescent, Jengod, Joelfurr, Jonathunder, Kumioko, LB-Versender, Lawrence King, Lemonsquares, LouI, Monegasque, Newyorkbrad, Nicke L, Nightkey, Nkrosse, North Shoreman, Nsaa, Omnedon, PJLazy, Quibik, Scott Mingus, ScottyBoy900Q, Seattledude, Settler, Tassedethe, The Mystery Man, TheKicker101, Thismightbezach, Tilden76, Tktru, Tom, TommyBoy, Uhai, Uris, User2004, VirginiaProp, VolatileChemical, WOSlinker, 24 anonymous edits ... 50

LeRoy Pope Walker *Source:* http://en.wikipedia.org/w/index.php?oldid=452965349 *License:* Creative Commons Attribution-Share Alike 3.0 Unported *Contributors:* A Werewolf, Caerwine, Complex01, DrDHMenke, Gobonobo, Hathawayc, Hlj, Hmains, Iridescent, Jengod, Jmlk17, JustAGal, Kumioko, LB-Versender, LonelyPilgrim, MattD1972, Omnedon, One, Pearle, Philip Stevens, Qst, RFD, Rich Farmbrough, RobertLunaIII, Scott Mingus, Searcher 1990, SpeDIt, The Mystery Man, Thismightbezach, Vianello, Walden69, Zoicon5, 11 anonymous edits ... 55

George W. Randolph *Source:* http://en.wikipedia.org/w/index.php?oldid=452965893 *License:* Creative Commons Attribution-Share Alike 3.0 Unported *Contributors:* AlexPlank, Caponer, Complex01, D6, Engines On, Fiftytwo thirty, Florian Huber, Hlj, Hmains, Itai, Jengod, Jobe6, Jun Nijo, Jwillbur, Kumioko, LB-Versender, Leodmacleod, MagnaMopus, Margo&Gladys, Mcelite, Melesse, Monegasque, Naerhu, Parkwells, Pauljeffersonks, Philip Stevens, Pigsonthewing, ProperlyRaised, Que-Can, Sadads, Scott Mingus, Searcher 1990, Seattledude, The Mystery Man, Thismightbezach, 15 anonymous edits ... 58

James Seddon *Source:* http://en.wikipedia.org/w/index.php?oldid=455772435 *License:* Creative Commons Attribution-Share Alike 3.0 Unported *Contributors:* AdamBMorgan, AlexPlank, Betacommand, Bill william compton, Catapult, Civil Engineer III, Complex01, D6, Darwinek, Davidcannon, Deville, Hlj, Hmains, Jengod, Ken Gallager, Kevin Myers, Kumioko, LB-Versender, Melesse, Minority Report, Philip Stevens, Plange, Plucas58, Popsracer, Qtoktok, Scott Mingus, Swvalaw, The Mystery Man, Thismightbezach, Warofdreams, Wknight94, 13 anonymous edits ... 61

John C. Breckinridge *Source:* http://en.wikipedia.org/w/index.php?oldid=457293986 *License:* Creative Commons Attribution-Share Alike 3.0 Unported *Contributors:* 8th Ohio Volunteers, A. Parrot, AJCham, AKGhetto, Abc85, Acdayrit, Acdixon, Aeusoes1, Agathman, AgnosticPreachersKid, Alex2706, Andrewhayes, ArcAngel, Ari Publican, Asiaticus, AzureCitizen, BD2412, Bedford, Ben76266, Berean Hunter, Billmckern, Billy Hathorn, Biruitorul, Brightwel, CJLL Wright, CWenger, Caponer, Chrisn4255, Connormah, Cyprian56, D Monack, DIDouglass, DLJessup, DanMS, Darolew, Darth Kalwejt, Davepape, Deleteme42, Dimadick, Dinosaur puppy, Docu, Dralwik, Dudeman5685, DwightKingsbury, Elipongo, Elliskev, Emperorbma, Ericl, Eyebum, Fat pig73, Flex, Foofighter20x, FourthAve, Fritz Saalfeld, G1076, GcSwRhIc, Glacier109, Golbez, GoldRingChip, Good Olfactory, GoodDay, Grandmasterka, Ground, Guthrum, Harryboyles, HennessyC, Hephaestos, Hlj, Hmains, IRP, Iamwisesun, Iglew, IgnorantArmies, Igoldste, J.delanoy, JForget, Jajhill, Japanese Searobin, JasonKitrick, JayJasper, Jengod, JimWae, Jjmillerhistorian, Jmlk17, John K, Jperrylsu, Jsferguson, Katharineamy, Kresock, KuatofKDY, Kumioko, LB-Versender, Lasy, LeaveSleaves, Lemonsquares, MK, Maximillion Pegasus, Mbr7975, Michael A. White, Minesweeper, Modocc, MrPrada, Nam, NawlinWiki, Neutrality, NewEnglandYankee, Newyorkbrad, NicoNet, Nikitko, Nobunaga24, North Shoreman, Nytimes19992000, Odysseyandoracle, OfficeBoy, Oxymoron83, Packerfansam, Pavel Vozenilek, Pdemeo, Philip Stevens, Pk97, Poulos2, Quadell, Quintote, Quuxplusone, RWReagan, RandySavageFTW, Recognizance, Reginald Perrin, Richard Arthur Norton (1958-), RickK, Rlquall, RobertLunaIII, Robertgreer, Robomanx, Rs09985, SDC, SLY111, ScathLann, Sciurinæ, Scott Mingus, Searcher 1990, Settler, ShelfSkewed, Slyfoxx, Soldan, Spacini, Stephennarmstrong, SteveSims, Stillstudying, Studerby, Tainter, Tassedethe, Tastywheat, Tedius Zanarukando, The Duke of Waltham, The Mystery Man, TheAznSensation, TheMidnighters, Theking17825, Thomas Gilling, Tiddly Tom, Tom, Trevour, Walden69, Webucation, Wierzba, William S. Saturn, Wjddbsals, Woohookitty, Zoe, 147 anonymous edits ... 63

Christopher Memminger *Source:* http://en.wikipedia.org/w/index.php?oldid=456724986 *License:* Creative Commons Attribution-Share Alike 3.0 Unported *Contributors:* Angleterre, Bender235, Bob Burkhardt, Complex01, Edward, Hmains, Jengod, Jmlk17, Jun Nijo, Kresspahl, Kumioko, LB-Versender, MK2, Monegasque, Omnedon, PaulHanson, Pwt898, RobertLunaIII, Scott Mingus, Seattledude, Tassedethe, The Mystery Man, Thismightbezach, TommyBoy, 7 anonymous edits ... 73

George Trenholm *Source:* http://en.wikipedia.org/w/index.php?oldid=444696926 *License:* Creative Commons Attribution-Share Alike 3.0 Unported *Contributors:* Auntof6, Can't sleep, clown will eat me, Chochopk, Crystallina, Da Stressor, Dharmabum420, Dr. E. Lee Spence, DuncanHill, Ground Zero, Gwu77, HunleyFinder, ILovePlankton, Inuhanyou838, Iwalters, Jabencarsey, Japanese Searobin, JimBobUSA, Joconnor, Jogers, Ka Faraq Gatri, Kumioko, LB-Versender, Martyman, MegX, Michael Devore, MishaPan, Omnedon, Ramroaster, RlyehRising, Shipwreckfan, The Mystery Man, Thismightbezach, TommyBoy, Zeamays, Zscout370, 13 anonymous edits ... 77

Judah P. Benjamin *Source:* http://en.wikipedia.org/w/index.php?oldid=457214664 *License:* Creative Commons Attribution-Share Alike 3.0 Unported *Contributors:* A Sniper, Adam keller, Adanumber, Anglius, AnnaFrance, Anne McDermott, Anythingyouwant, Archanamiya, Asparagirl, B.Wind, BD2412, Barticus88, Baxterguy, Bearcat, Bender235, Bigsean0300, Billy Hathorn, Bob Wallace, BocoROTH, C. C. Perez, Chzz, Civil Engineer III, Clariosophic, Cliftonian, Complex01, CutOffTies, D6, DO'Neil, Darth Kalwejt, Davshul, Dirkbb, Dosimmon, DuncanHill, Eastmain, Elipitz, Fat&Happy, Flora68, Floydspinky71, G.-M. Cupertino, Gaius Cornelius, Good Olfactory, Gruepig, Hephaestos, Herbm1, Horologium, IZAK, Infrogmation, Ismoot, Jack Merridew, Jack O'Lantern, JamesMLane, Jengod, Jmlk17, Joal Beal, John K, Johnbibby, Johnpacklambert, Jorge Stolfi, Jpcarver, Kbdank71, Kingstowngalway, KuatofKDY, Kumioko, LADBROOKE, LB-Versender, Levineps, Lisa, Lockley, MK2, Malik Shabazz, Masterpiece2000, Mattbr, Mav, Mdmace91, MikeLynch, Miranche, Mmcknight4, Myles Alderman, Mysdaao, Narzos, Neutrality, Nhl4hamilton, Nightkey, Nytimes19992000, Ogress, Onesius, Packerfansam, Parkwells, Petey Parrot, Philip Stevens, Phreddd, Pilot1413, Piratedan, Prinzwilhelm, QuartierLatin1968, R613vlu, Rdsmith4, Rettetast, Richard David Ramsey, Rockenonboy, Satori Son, SchfiftyThree, Scott Mingus, Seattledude, Ser Amantio di Nicolao, Serte, Sf46, Shamir1, Shooterwalker, SidP, Smessick, Steven J. Anderson, TCY, TPIRFanSteve, The Mystery Man, The Ogre, The Special Education Squad, Thismightbezach, Thoreaulylazy, TomPhil, Tomas417, Twelfthian, Versus22, Vulturell, WCCasey, Walden69, Wassermann, WikiFlier, Wknight94, Y, YeshuaDavid, Youfamissim, Youngamerican, Yworo, Zoe, 111 anonymous edits ... 79

Thomas Bragg *Source:* http://en.wikipedia.org/w/index.php?oldid=444699647 *License:* Creative Commons Attribution-Share Alike 3.0 Unported *Contributors:* Antandrus, Awbeal, BD2412, Benfergy, Canuckian89, Complex01, D6, Darth Kalwejt, Desk Jockey, Ebear422, FeanorStar7, Floydspinky71, Golbez, Good Olfactory, Hmains, HollyAm, Jack Cox, KuatofKDY, Kumioko, LB-Versender, Lemonsquares, Mattbr, Mechla, Mikehelms, Monegasque, Omnedon, RogDel, Sardanaphalus, Scott Mingus, Seth Ilys, The Mystery Man, The Special Education Squad, Thismightbezach, Tom, TommyBoy, Vclaw, Willthacheerleader18, Youfamissim, Zaphod Beeblebrox, 9 anonymous edits ... 89

Thomas H. Watts *Source:* http://en.wikipedia.org/w/index.php?oldid=452289575 *License:* Creative Commons Attribution-Share Alike 3.0 Unported *Contributors:* Bearcat, BrownHairedGirl, Bte99, Cenantua, Charles Matthews, Complex01, Connormah, D6, Danny, Darth Kalwejt, Everyking, GhostPirate, Gilliam, Golbez, GoodDay, Grutness, Hmains, HollyAm, Iwalters, Jack Cox, JamesAM, Jcp3151, Jetman, JodyB, Kumioko, LB-Versender, Mattbr, MrDolomite, RobStreatham, Sardanaphalus, Scewing, Scott Mingus, The Mystery Man, Thismightbezach, Ulric1313, 4 anonymous edits ... 91

George Davis (politician) *Source:* http://en.wikipedia.org/w/index.php?oldid=452701673 *License:* Creative Commons Attribution-Share Alike 3.0 Unported *Contributors:* Bazj, Bellhalla, BrownHairedGirl, Bunnyhop11, Clarityfiend, Complex01, Darth Kalwejt, EchetusXe, Fat pig73, GhostPirate, Hmains, Jaxl, Jengod, Jmlk17, Kumioko, LB-Versender, Magnus Manske, Mattbr, MiniGamer, MisfitToys, Ohconfucius, Omnedon, RSStockdale, Rbraunwa, Rupertslander, Ruud Koot, Scott Mingus, TarHippo, The Mystery Man, Thismightbezach, Tktru, TommyBoy, WOSlinker, Wildhartlivie, 4 anonymous edits ... 93

John Henninger Reagan *Source:* http://en.wikipedia.org/w/index.php?oldid=456208447 *License:* Creative Commons Attribution-Share Alike 3.0 Unported *Contributors:* Angusmclellan, Argos'Dad, Badbilltucker, Badmachine, Bellhalla, Bms4880, CSWarren, Canuckian89, Catapult, Claffey27, Complex01, Davepape, Dralwik, Dugwiki, Dumelow, Eastlaw, Edton, Floydspinky71, Friedo, GJeffery, GoingBatty, Good Olfactory, Gwillhickers, Hedgey42, Hmains, Hugo999, JCarriker, Jengod, Jmlk17, Junglecat, Kingpin13, KuatofKDY, Kumioko, LB-Versender, LarryJeff, Ling.Nut, Maile66, Maltmomma, Maverick9711, Meelar, MishaPan, Moestue, Monegasque, Neilc, Neutrality, Paul Benjamin Austin, PedanticallySpeaking, R'n'B, RSStockdale, RadicalBender, Redwolf24, Reywas92, Rich Farmbrough, Richard Arthur Norton (1958-), RobertLunaIII, Scimitar, Scott Mingus, Ser Amantio di Nicolao, Shangrilaista, Slambo, Storm Rider, Studerby, Tabletop, The Mystery Man, The wub, Thismightbezach, Tom, Unyoyega, Walden69, Wasbeer, WhisperToMe, Woodsstock, 23 anonymous edits ... 97

Stephen Mallory *Source:* http://en.wikipedia.org/w/index.php?oldid=453639102 *License:* Creative Commons Attribution-Share Alike 3.0 Unported *Contributors:* 15lsoucy, AlexandrDmitri, Alvestrand, Badbilltucker, Bobblewik, Civil Engineer III, Complex01, Connormah, D6, Darwinek, Descendall, Disavian, EdH, Emmo827, Emperor001, Eric Herboso, Floydspinky71, Gaius Cornelius, Gamaliel, GcSwRhIc, Gizmoandalice, Good Olfactory, Ground Zero, Guettarda, Hephaestos, Hmains, Ian Rose, Infrogmation, JASpencer, JTRH, Jengod, Jmlk17, John K, Johnpacklambert, Joyous!, Khatru2, Koavf, KuatofKDY, Kumioko, LB-Versender, LeonidasSpartan, Maralia, McMullen, NameIsRon, Nathcer, Nuggetboy, Oxmn9, Packerfansam, Pkkphysicist, Plange, Scott Mingus, Sturmvogel 66, The Mystery Man, Thismightbezach, Tom, Ugen64, Vini 175, WereSpielChequers, WhiskyWhiskers, Woohookitty, Youfamissim, 13 anonymous edits ... 105

Image Sources, Licenses and Contributors

The sources listed for each image provide more detailed licensing information including the copyright status, the copyright owner, and the license conditions.

Image *Source:* http://en.wikipedia.org/w/index.php?title=File:Jefferson_Davis_1853_daguerreotype.png *License:* Public Domain *Contributors:* unattributed ... 3

Image *Source:* http://en.wikipedia.org/w/index.php?title=File:Jefferson_Davis_Signature.svg *License:* Public Domain *Contributors:* Jefferson Davis, digitalization by Connormah ... 4

Image *Source:* http://en.wikipedia.org/w/index.php?title=File:Confederate_National_Flag_since_Mar_4_1865.svg *License:* Public Domain *Contributors:* Fornax, Fry1989, Homo lupus, O, Pmsyyz, Sceptic, Vantey, 2 anonymous edits ... 4

Image *Source:* http://en.wikipedia.org/w/index.php?title=File:US_flag_34_stars.svg *License:* Public Domain *Contributors:* Homo lupus, Jacobolus, Wikiborg, Zscout370, 3 anonymous edits ... 4

Figure 1 *Source:* http://en.wikipedia.org/w/index.php?title=File:Sarah_Knox_Taylor.jpg *License:* Public Domain *Contributors:* Frank C. Müller, PhilFree, 1 anonymous edits ... 7

Figure 2 *Source:* http://en.wikipedia.org/w/index.php?title=File:VHowellDavis.jpg *License:* Public Domain *Contributors:* The Mystery Man ... 8

Figure 3 *Source:* http://en.wikipedia.org/w/index.php?title=File:Winnie_Davis_001.jpg *License:* Public Domain *Contributors:* The American monthly review ... 9

Figure 4 *Source:* http://en.wikipedia.org/w/index.php?title=File:1861_Davis_Inaugural.jpg *License:* Public Domain *Contributors:* Archibald Crossland McIntyre of Montgomery, Alabama ... 12

Figure 5 *Source:* http://en.wikipedia.org/w/index.php?title=File:J_Davis_1861-5c.jpg *License:* Public Domain *Contributors:* Confederate Post Office, 1861 ... 12

Figure 6 *Source:* http://en.wikipedia.org/w/index.php?title=File:ConfederateCabinet.jpg *License:* Public Domain *Contributors:* Harper's Weekly. Original uploader was The Mystery Man at en.wikipedia ... 14

Figure 7 *Source:* http://en.wikipedia.org/w/index.php?title=File:William_T_Sutherlin_Mansion_Danville_Virginia.JPG *License:* Creative Commons Attribution-Sharealike 3.0 *Contributors:* MarmadukePercy ... 17

Figure 8 *Source:* http://en.wikipedia.org/w/index.php?title=File:Jefferson_davis_fort_monroe_capture.jpg *License:* Public Domain *Contributors:* Waud, Alfred R ... 18

Figure 9 *Source:* http://en.wikipedia.org/w/index.php?title=File:1885JeffersonDavis.jpg *License:* Public Domain *Contributors:* Centennial Photographic Co. ... 19

Figure 10 *Source:* http://en.wikipedia.org/w/index.php?title=File:Jefferson_Davis_portrait.jpg *License:* Public Domain *Contributors:* Original uploader was The Mystery Man at en.wikipedia ... 20

Image *Source:* http://en.wikipedia.org/w/index.php?title=File:Howell_Cobb-crop.jpg *License:* Public Domain *Contributors:* Connormah, Homo lupus 25

Figure 11 *Source:* http://en.wikipedia.org/w/index.php?title=File:Buchanan_Cabinet.jpg *License:* Public Domain *Contributors:* Original uploader was The Mystery Man at en.wikipedia ... 28

Figure 12 *Source:* http://en.wikipedia.org/w/index.php?title=File:Postbellum-Cobb.jpg *License:* Public Domain *Contributors:* Brady-Handy Photograph Collection (Library of Congress) ... 30

Image *Source:* http://en.wikipedia.org/w/index.php?title=File:PD-icon.svg *License:* Public Domain *Contributors:* Alex.muller, Anomie, Anonymous Dissident, CBM, MBisanz, Quadell, Rocket000, Strangerer, Timotheus Canens, 1 anonymous edits ... 31

Image *Source:* http://en.wikipedia.org/w/index.php?title=File:Alexander_Stephens_-1855.jpg *License:* Public Domain *Contributors:* unknown . 33

Image *Source:* http://en.wikipedia.org/w/index.php?title=File:Alexander_Stephens_Signature.svg *License:* Public Domain *Contributors:* Connormah, Alexander Stephens ... 34

Figure 13 *Source:* http://en.wikipedia.org/w/index.php?title=File:Alexander_Stephens.jpg *License:* Public Domain *Contributors:* Original uploader was The Mystery Man at en.wikipedia ... 37

Figure 14 *Source:* http://en.wikipedia.org/w/index.php?title=File:ConfederateCabinet.jpg *License:* Public Domain *Contributors:* Harper's Weekly. Original uploader was The Mystery Man at en.wikipedia ... 38

Figure 15 *Source:* http://en.wikipedia.org/w/index.php?title=File:AlexStephens2.jpg *License:* Public Domain *Contributors:* Brady-Handy Photograph Collection (Library of Congress). Cropped by The Mystery Man at en.wikipedia ... 39

Figure 16 *Source:* http://en.wikipedia.org/w/index.php?title=File:John_White_Alexander_-_Alexander_Stephens_portrait.jpg *License:* Public Domain *Contributors:* John White Alexander ... 40

Figure 17 *Source:* http://en.wikipedia.org/w/index.php?title=File:Stephens_Monument.JPG *License:* GNU Free Documentation License *Contributors:* Original uploader was Ezratrumpet at en.wikipedia ... 41

Image *Source:* http://en.wikipedia.org/w/index.php?title=File:Robert_Toombs_-_Brady-Handy.jpg *License:* Public Domain *Contributors:* (1823-1896) or Levin Handy (1855-1932) ... 43

Figure 18 *Source:* http://en.wikipedia.org/w/index.php?title=File:Rob_Toombs.jpg *License:* Public Domain *Contributors:* Grendelkhan, Väsk . 45

Figure 19 *Source:* http://en.wikipedia.org/w/index.php?title=File:ConfederateCabinet.jpg *License:* Public Domain *Contributors:* Harper's Weekly. Original uploader was The Mystery Man at en.wikipedia ... 47

Figure 20 *Source:* http://en.wikipedia.org/w/index.php?title=File:Robert_Toombs_House,_(Wilkes_County,_Georgia).jpg *License:* Public Domain *Contributors:* Branan Sanders, Photographer ... 48

Image *Source:* http://en.wikipedia.org/w/index.php?title=File:RbrtMTHntr.jpg *License:* Public Domain *Contributors:* Brady, Mathew B., 1823 (ca.)-1896. Original uploader was The Mystery Man at en.wikipedia ... 50

Figure 21 *Source:* http://en.wikipedia.org/w/index.php?title=File:RMTH-standingright.jpg *License:* Public Domain *Contributors:* Magog the Ogre, Quibik ... 52

Figure 22 *Source:* http://en.wikipedia.org/w/index.php?title=File:Robert_M._T._Hunter_c1865.jpg *License:* Public Domain *Contributors:* Jbarta, Quibik ... 53

Image *Source:* http://en.wikipedia.org/w/index.php?title=File:Walker,_Leroy_Pope_1.jpg *License:* Copyrighted free use *Contributors:* Edelseider, Homo lupus, Kramer Associates, LB-Versender ... 55

Figure 23 *Source:* http://en.wikipedia.org/w/index.php?title=File:ConfederateCabinet.jpg *License:* Public Domain *Contributors:* Harper's Weekly. Original uploader was The Mystery Man at en.wikipedia ... 57

Image *Source:* http://en.wikipedia.org/w/index.php?title=File:George_Wythe_Randolph_1.jpg *License:* Public Domain *Contributors:* Docu, Frank C. Müller, Homo lupus, Julius Morton, LB-Versender ... 58

Image *Source:* http://en.wikipedia.org/w/index.php?title=File:James_Alexander_Seddon_1.jpg *License:* GNU Free Documentation License *Contributors:* Billinghurst, Kilom691, LB-Versender ... 61

Image *Source:* http://en.wikipedia.org/w/index.php?title=File:John_C_Breckinridge-04775-restored.jpg *License:* Public Domain *Contributors:* .Retouching by AJCham. ... 63

Image *Source:* http://en.wikipedia.org/w/index.php?title=File:BreckinridgeSignature.svg *License:* Public Domain *Contributors:* Connormah, John C. Breckinridge ... 64

Image *Source:* http://en.wikipedia.org/w/index.php?title=File:CSAGeneral.png *License:* Public Domain *Contributors:* Original uploader was CaptainMike at en.wikipedia ... 64

Figure 24 *Source:* http://en.wikipedia.org/w/index.php?title=File:JCBreckinridge.jpg *License:* Public Domain *Contributors:* The Mystery Man .65

Figure 25 *Source:* http://en.wikipedia.org/w/index.php?title=File:General_John_C_Breckinridge.jpg *License:* Public Domain *Contributors:* Himasaram, Masturbius, Nobunaga24, WTCA, Walden69 ... 68

Figure 26 *Source:* http://en.wikipedia.org/w/index.php?title=File:John_C._Breckinridge_statue_Lexington_KY.jpg *License:* Public Domain *Contributors:* Hlj ... 68

Figure 27 *Source:* http://en.wikipedia.org/w/index.php?title=File:JCBreckinridge-postbellum.jpg *License:* Public Domain *Contributors:* Beao, Jbarta, The Mystery Man ... 70

Figure 28 *Source:* http://en.wikipedia.org/w/index.php?title=File:John_C._Breckinridge_grave.jpg *License:* Public Domain *Contributors:* Bedford 70

Image *Source:* http://en.wikipedia.org/w/index.php?title=File:CGM.jpg *License:* Public Domain *Contributors:* Author died more than 70 years ago 73

Figure 29 *Source:* http://en.wikipedia.org/w/index.php?title=File:ConfederateCabinet.jpg *License:* Public Domain *Contributors:* Harper's Weekly. Original uploader was The Mystery Man at en.wikipedia 75
Image *Source:* http://en.wikipedia.org/w/index.php?title=File:GATrenholm.jpg *License:* Public Domain *Contributors:* Original uploader was The Mystery Man at en.wikipedia 77
Image *Source:* http://en.wikipedia.org/w/index.php?title=File:Gamble_Plantation_Judah.P.Benjamin_Photo.JPG *License:* Public Domain *Contributors:* Jwgloverii 79
Figure 30 *Source:* http://en.wikipedia.org/w/index.php?title=File:JPBenjamin.jpg *License:* Public Domain *Contributors:* Unknown. 82
Figure 31 *Source:* http://en.wikipedia.org/w/index.php?title=File:ConfederateCabinet.jpg *License:* Public Domain *Contributors:* Harper's Weekly. Original uploader was The Mystery Man at en.wikipedia 83
Figure 32 *Source:* http://en.wikipedia.org/w/index.php?title=File:Judah_Benjamin.jpg *License:* Public Domain *Contributors:* Himasaram, Howcheng, Walden69 85
Figure 33 *Source:* http://en.wikipedia.org/w/index.php?title=File:Jpb_grave.jpg *License:* Creative Commons Attribution-Sharealike 3.0 *Contributors:* NYC JD 86
Image *Source:* http://en.wikipedia.org/w/index.php?title=File:Thomas_Bragg_1.jpg *License:* GNU Free Documentation License *Contributors:* LBVersender, Man vyi, Scooter 89
Image *Source:* http://en.wikipedia.org/w/index.php?title=File:Thomas_Hill_Watts_1860s.jpg *License:* Public Domain *Contributors:* unattributed 91
Image *Source:* http://en.wikipedia.org/w/index.php?title=File:George_Davis.jpg *License:* Public Domain *Contributors:* Original uploader was Ghost-Pirate at en.wikipedia 93
Image *Source:* http://en.wikipedia.org/w/index.php?title=File:JHReagan.jpg *License:* Public Domain *Contributors:* Unknown. Original uploader was The Mystery Man at en.wikipedia 97
Figure 34 *Source:* http://en.wikipedia.org/w/index.php?title=File:ConfederateCabinet.jpg *License:* Public Domain *Contributors:* Harper's Weekly. Original uploader was The Mystery Man at en.wikipedia 99
Figure 35 *Source:* http://en.wikipedia.org/w/index.php?title=File:John_Henninger_Reagan.jpg *License:* Public Domain *Contributors:* Nv8200p, Scooter 101
Figure 36 *Source:* http://en.wikipedia.org/w/index.php?title=File:ReaganStateoffBuildAustinTX.JPG *License:* Public Domain *Contributors:* WhisperToMe 102
Image *Source:* http://en.wikipedia.org/w/index.php?title=File:Steph_mallory.jpg *License:* Public Domain *Contributors:* Howcheng, Tendsprice Bradford 105
Figure 37 *Source:* http://en.wikipedia.org/w/index.php?title=File:ConfederateCabinet.jpg *License:* Public Domain *Contributors:* Harper's Weekly. Original uploader was The Mystery Man at en.wikipedia 111
Image *Source:* http://en.wikipedia.org/w/index.php?title=File:Wikisource-logo.svg *License:* logo *Contributors:* Nicholas Moreau 119

License

Creative Commons Attribution-Share Alike 3.0 Unported
//creativecommons.org/licenses/by-sa/3.0/

Index

Abbeville, South Carolina, 117
Abolitionist, 74, 82, 87
Abraham Lincoln, 5, 47, 51, 52, 59, 64, 74, 86, 110
Acquittal, 35
Acting Vice President, 28
Adelbert Ames, 4
Admission to the bar in the United States, 65
African Americans, 18
A. H. Stephens Historic Park, 41
Alabama, 56, 91
Alabama House of Representatives, 92
Alabama State Capitol, 12
Alabama Territory, 91
Albert G. Brown, 10
Alexander H.H. Stuart, 59
Alexander H. Stephens, **33**, 45, 46
Alexander Keith Marshall, 63
Alexander Stephen and Sons, 33
Alexander Stephens, 3, 13, 28, 47, 57, 75, 83, 93, 99, 100, 111
Alfred H. Colquitt, 33
Alma mater, 4, 26, 44, 51, 64, 80, 93
Alternate history, 87
Ambrose R. Wright, 41
American Civil War, 5, 27, 34, 44, 58, 61, 64, 66, 77, 89–91, 106, 107
American Revolutionary War, 6
Anderson County, Texas, 98
Andersonville prison, 29
Andrew Jackson, 27
Andrew Johnson, 106, 117
Annexation of Texas, 46
Anti-Catholic, 37
Appletons Cyclopædia of American Biography, 130
Arlington County, Virginia, 21
Army of Northern Virginia, 13, 27, 29, 48, 67, 100
Army of Tennessee, 67
Army of the Potomac, 100
Army of the Potomac (Confederate), 48
A Short History of the Confederate States of America, 19

Athens, Georgia, 27, 31, 35, 44
Atlanta Campaign, 29
Atlanta, Georgia, 34
Attempted murder, 35
Attorney General, 83, 89, 90, 92–94
Attorney General of the United States, 59
Austin, Texas, 99

Bahamas, 85
Bar (law), 44
Barrister, 80, 86
Baton Rouge, 130
Baton Rouge, Louisiana, 128, 129
Battle of Antietam, 14, 29, 48
Battle of Big Bethel, 59
Battle of Buena Vista, 9
Battle of Chickamauga, 67
Battle of Cold Harbor, 67
Battle of Columbus, Georgia, 30
Battle of Forts Jackson and St. Philip, 114
Battle of Fort Stevens, 67
Battle of Gettysburg, 14, 40, 100
Battle of Hampton Roads, 114
Battle of Missionary Ridge, 67
Battle of Monocacy, 67
Battle of New Market, 64, 67
Battle of Roanoke Island, 84
Battle of Saltville I, 69
Battle of Shiloh, 67
Battle of South Mountain, 29
Battle of Stones River, 67
Beauvoir (Biloxi, Mississippi), 18
Belle Chasse, Louisiana, 81
Ben H. Procter, 102
Benjamin Disraeli, 130
Benjamin Huger (1805-1877), 84
Benjamin Wade, 82
Ben Montgomery, 17
Bennett Place, 69
Bimini, 85
Biographical Directory of the United States Congress, 23, 31, 42, 49, 53, 62, 71, 88, 103, 131
Black Hawk (Sauk leader), 6

Black Hawk War, 6
Boardinghouse, 107
Border states (American Civil War), 66
Boston, 11
Boston Harbor, 40
Boston, Massachusetts, 100
Braxton Bragg, 15, 16, 67, 89
Breckenridge, Colorado, 69
Breckenridge, Minnesota, 69
Breckenridge, Missouri, 69
Breckenridge, Texas, 69
Breckinridge family, 64
Bridgeport, Connecticut, 118
Brierfield Plantation, 7
Brigade, 10, 29
Brigadier general, 48, 56
Brigadier General (CSA), 66
Brigadier general (United States), 10, 29, 59
British subject, 80
British West Indies, 105, 107
Buffalo, Texas, 99
Bunny Breckinridge, 64
Burlington, Iowa, 65

Cabinet (government), 80
Cadet, 64
California, 46
Cambridge, Massachusetts, 59
Canada, 49, 69
Capital punishment, 35
Carl Sandburg, 82
Casemate, 17
Catholic Encyclopedia, 119
Catholicism, 106
Cathy Young, 128
Cedar Key, Florida, 17
Censure, 84
Centre College, 64, 65
Charles Francis Adams, Sr., 115
Charles Magill Conrad, 3
Charles M. Conrad, 117
Charles Morehead, 63
Charles Stewart (Texas politician), 98
Charleston, South Carolina, 13, 51, 74, 77, 81
Charlotte, North Carolina, 117
Charlottesville, Virginia, 44, 58, 59
Chattanooga, Tennessee, 67
Christian County, Kentucky, 4, 6
Christiansted, U.S. Virgin Islands, 80
Christopher Memminger, 14, 38, 47, 57, **73**, 77, 78, 83, 99, 111
Cincinnatus, 101
Cirrhosis, 69
Clement C. Clay, 116
Clement Claiborne Clay, 14
Clifton Rodes Breckinridge, 64

Colonel, 59
Colonel (United States), 4, 29, 48
Colonist, 59
Columbus, Georgia, 30
Committee on Finance, 51
Compromise of 1850, 10, 28, 36, 46
Conclusion of the American Civil War, 16
Confederate Congress, 38
Confederate Constitution, 75
Confederate privateer, 113
Confederate Provisional Congress, 29
Confederate settlements in British Honduras, 86
Confederate States, 112
Confederate States Army, 13, 27, 29, 30, 44, 48, 56, 64, 66
Confederate States Attorney General, 79, 94
Confederate States Navy, 105
Confederate States of America, 4, 5, 27, 34, 38, 47, 59, 66, 74, 77, 80, 89, 90, 93, 94, 98, 106
Confederate States of America dollar, 41, 60, 73, 76, 77, 85, 98
Confederate States of America Post-office Department, 100
Confederate States Secretary of State, 43, 47, 50, 52, 79, 84
Confederate States Secretary of the Navy, 111
Confederate States Secretary of War, 55, 56, 58, 60, 61, 63, 64, 69, 79, 83
Congress of the Confederate States, 51, 94
Congress of the United States, 61
Conscription, 40
Constitutional Union Party (United States), 34–36, 66
Continental Army, 6
Copyright status of work by the U.S. government, 31, 54
Cornelius Vanderbilt, 18
Cornerstone Speech, 39
Crawfordville, Georgia, 34, 45
Crawford W. Long, 35
C.S.A.: The Confederate States of America, 87
CSS Alabama, 115, 132
CSS Albemarle, 116
CSS Arkansas, 114
CSS David, 116
CSS Florida (cruiser), 115, 132
CSS Georgia (cruiser), 115, 132
CSS H. L. Hunley, 116
CSS Louisiana, 114
CSS Manassas, 132
CSS Mississippi, 114
CSS Nashville (1861), 132
CSS Shenandoah, 115, 132

142

CSS Sumter, 113, 132
CSS Tennessee (1862), 114
CSS Virginia, 114, 132
Cuba, 10, 49, 69

Dallas County, Alabama, 91
Daniel Huntington, 20
Danish West Indies, 80, 81
Danville, Kentucky, 65
Danville, Virginia, 16, 117
Dara Horn, 87
David B. Culberson, 97
David J. Eicher, 71
David Levy Yulee, 17, 81, 108
David L. Yulee, 81, 111
David Rumph Jones, 48
Davis Bend, Mississippi, 7
Declaration of Independence, 59
Declaration of the Immediate Causes Which Induce and Justify the Secession of South Carolina from the Federal Union, 75
Deep South, 36, 66
Delaware, 66
Democratic Party (United States), 4, 5, 26, 34, 44, 51, 56, 58, 61, 64, 65, 74, 77, 80, 82, 89, 91, 93, 98, 105
Demosthenian Literary Society, 44
Diphtheria, 9
Division (military), 48
Dix-Hill Cartel, 29
Dominican Order, 6
Dred Scott v. Sandford, 38
Duel, 82

Earl of Stirling, 61
Earl Van Dorn, 15
Eastern Theater of the American Civil War, 67
Edmund J. Davis, 101
Edmund Kirby Smith, 15
Edmund Randolph, 59
Edward Junius Black, 26
Edwin M. Stanton, 118
Eggnog Riot, 6
Electoral College (United States), 38, 64
Ellenton, Florida, 85
Encyclopædia Britannica Eleventh Edition, 31, 54
Encyclopedia Americana, 130
England, 89
English Bill, 46
Episcopal Church (United States), 4, 58, 74
Essex County, Virginia, 51
Estate (land), 17
Ethelbert Barksdale, 116
Executive, 38, 47, 57, 75, 83, 99, 111

Expulsion from the United States Congress, 52, 66, 90

Fairview, Christian County, Kentucky, 21
Falmouth, Virginia, 61
Faneuil Hall, 11
Father, 59
Fayetteville Academy, 81
Federal government of the United States, 10
Federal Highway Administration, 128
Felix Huston Robertson, 69
Fiat money, 75
Filibuster (military), 10
Find a Grave, 31, 53, 60, 62, 71, 95, 103, 127, 129, 131
Fire-eaters, 108
First Corps, Army of Northern Virginia, 100
First Transcontinental Railroad, 11
Flat Rock, Henderson County, North Carolina, 76
Florida, 69, 106
Fort Crawford, 6
Fort Hamilton, 94
Fort Monroe, 17
Fort Pickens, 39
Fort Pulaski, 78
Fort Sumter, 13, 39
Fort Warren (Massachusetts), 40, 100
Francis H. Cone, 36
Francis R. Lubbock, 100
Franklin College of Arts and Sciences, 44
Franklin Pierce, 3, 5, 65, 82
French Creole, 81
Fugitive Slave Law, 38

Gadsden Purchase, 11
Gamble Plantation Historic State Park, 85
Garrett Davis, 63
Gatlinburg, Tennessee, 98
General, 89
General (CSA), 67
General officer, 44, 64
General ticket, 26
George A. Trenholm, 100
George Davis (politician), 15, **93**
George G. Meade, 100
George R. Davis, 93
Georgetown, Kentucky, 65
George Trenholm, 15, 73, 76, **77**, 98
George Washington, 59
George W. Crawford, 26
George W. Randolph, 15, **58**, 61, 79
George W. Towns, 26
George W. Whitmore, 98
George Wythe, 59
Georgia House of Representatives, 35, 44

143

Georgia Platform, 28, 36, 46
Georgias 6th congressional district, 26
Georgias 8th congressional district, 34
Georgias At-large congressional district, 26
Georgia State Senate, 35
Georgia (U.S. state), 26, 34, 43, 78
Germany, 74
Gerrit Smith, 18
Gideon Welles, 113
Given Campbell, 16
Goochland County, Virginia, 61
Governor of Alabama, 91, 92
Governor of Georgia, 26, 29, 33
Governor of Louisiana, 20
Governor of New Jersey, 8
Governor of North Carolina, 89
Governor of Texas, 100
Gray Victory, 87
Greensboro, North Carolina, 16, 117
Greenville, Alabama, 91
Gustavus Woodson Smith, 48

Habeas corpus, 39
Hampton Roads Conference, 40, 52
Handbook of Texas, 103
Hannibal Hamlin, 63, 66
Harry Turtledove, 87
Havana, 16
Henderson County, Texas, 99
Henry A. Wise, 84
Henry Clay, 46
Henry S. Foote, 116
Henry Stuart Foote, 10
Henry T. Ellett, 4
Herschel Vespasian Johnson, 26
Herschel V. Johnson, 47
Historical regions of the United States, 28
Historical Society of Pennsylvania, 42
Historic Oakwood Cemetery, 90
History of Confederate States Army Generals, 64
History of the United States, 98
Hollywood Cemetery (Richmond, Virginia), 20
Homer V.M. Miller, 43
Horace Chilton, 97
Horace Greeley, 18
Howell Cobb, 13, **25**, 36, 46
Howell Cobb (Elder), 31
Human eye, 11
Hunter Davidson, 116
Huntsville, Alabama, 55, 56
Hurricane Katrina, 21

Illinois, 38
Immigrant, 37

Impressment, 39
Income tax, 75
Interstate Commerce Commission, 101
Irwin County, Georgia, 16
Irwinville, Georgia, 16, 100
Isaac Toucey, 28

Jackson, Mississippi, 10
Jackson, North Carolina, 89
Jacob Thompson, 28
James Archibald Meriwether, 26
James Buchanan, 11, 26–28, 37, 63, 66
James D. Bulloch, 115
James Guthrie (American politician), 26
James H. North, 115
James K. Polk, 8, 10, 27, 45, 46, 50
James River, 114
James River (Virginia), 62
James S. Boynton, 33
James Seddon, 58, **61**, 63
James Stephen Hogg, 102
Jefferson College (Washington, Mississippi), 4, 6
Jefferson County, Georgia, 26, 27
Jefferson Davis, **3**, 26, 27, 33, 38, 39, 47, 50, 52, 55, 57, 58, 60, 61, 63, 69, 75, 79, 80, 82, 83, 90, 92–94, 98–100, 106, 111
Jefferson Davis Memorial Highway, 21
Jefferson Davis Presidential Library, 21
Jefferson Davis State Historic Site, 21
Jefferson Literary and Debating Society, 51
Jeremiah S. Black, 28
Jesse Speight, 4, 10
Jew, 80
Jim Hogg, 101
John Archibald Campbell, 13
John Bell Hood, 16
John Bell (Tennessee politician), 66
John B. Floyd, 3
John Breckinridge (Attorney General), 64
John Brown (abolitionist), 18, 74
John Buchanan Floyd, 3
John C. Breckinridge, 15, 47, 61, **63**
John C. Breckinridge Memorial, 71
John C. Calhoun, 46
John Dickson Carr, 87
John D. Winters, 130
John Gill Shorter, 91, 92
John Henninger Reagan, 14, 38, 47, 57, 75, 77, 83, **97**, 111
John James Jones, 34
John J. Crittenden, 63
John J. McRae, 4
John J. Pettus, 11
John L. Porter, 112
John Marie Durst, 99

John Mercer Brooke, 116
John Roane, 50
John Rolfe, 59
John S. Carlile, 50
John White (Kentucky politician), 50
John Williams Walker, 56
Joseph E. Brown, 47
Joseph E. Johnston, 13, 16, 69, 100
Joseph Holt, 28
Jubal Early, 67
Judah P. Benjamin, 14, 38, 47, 51, 55, 57, 58, 75, **79**, 89, 99, 111, 132
Judaism, 80
Judge, 105
Julius Caesar Alford, 26
July 4, 11
Junius Hillyer, 26

Kansas, 46
Kansas-Nebraska Act, 36, 46
Kansas Territory, 37
Kaufman County, Texas, 99
Kentucky, 4, 63, 64
Kentucky House of Representatives, 65
Kentucky in the American Civil War, 66
Kentucky Legislature, 66
Kentuckys 8th congressional district, 63
Key West, 94
Key West, Florida, 107
Klein, 128
Know Nothing, 99
Know-Nothing movement, 99
Know-Nothing Party, 37
Ku Klux Klan, 69

La Grange, Georgia, 117
Law, 26, 51
Lawyer, 34, 44, 58, 61, 74, 80, 89, 98, 105
Lecompton Constitution, 37, 46, 110
Lemuel D. Evans, 98
LeRoy Pope, 56
LeRoy Pope Walker, 14, 38, 47, **55**, 75, 79, 83, 99, 111
Levin Corbin Handy, 63
Lewis Cass, 28
Lewis E. Parsons, 91
Lexington Cemetery, 69
Lexington History Center, 68
Lexington, Kentucky, 6, 64, 65
Lexington, Virginia, 64
Liberty Hall (Crawfordville, Georgia), 41
Liberty ship, 52, 94
Library of Congress, 128
Lieutenant General (CSA), 67
Linn Boyd, 25
List of Governors of Alabama, 91

List of Governors of Georgia, 27, 34
List of Governors of North Carolina, 89
List of Governors of Texas, 101
List of Vice Presidents of the United States, 63, 64
Lloyds, Virginia, 52
London, 49
Lord John Russell, 115
Lott Warren, 26
Louisiana, 4, 64, 80
Louisiana Historical Association, 20
Louisiana House of Representatives, 80
Louisiana State University, 129
Louisiana State University Press, 128, 130
Louisville and Nashville Railroad, 20
Louisville, Kentucky, 7
Lyons, Georgia, 49

M1841 Mississippi Rifle, 9
Macon, Georgia, 30
Major, 59
Major General (CSA), 66
Major general (United States), 27, 29
Major (United States), 65
Malaria, 7
Mansion, 17
Maple Hill Cemetery (Huntsville, Alabama), 57
Mark A. Cooper, 35
Mark Anthony Cooper, 26, 34
Martha Jefferson Randolph, 58, 59
Martin Van Buren, 50
Maryland, 66
Maryland Campaign, 48
Mathew Brady, 63
Matthew Fontaine Maury, 109
Memminger, Charles Gustavus, 130
Memminger, Christopher Gustavus, 130
Memorial Day, 21
Memphis, Tennessee, 18
Metairie Cemetery, 20
Methodist, 44, 98
Mexican-American War, 4, 5, 28, 36, 46
Mexican-American War, 64, 65
Mexico, 36
Midshipman, 59
Militia, 10, 48
Millard Fillmore, 25, 28, 51, 82, 108
Mississippi, 3, 5, 82
Mississippis At-large congressional district, 4
Mississippi Valley, 67
Missouri, 66
Missouri Compromise, 36
Mixed-race, 87
Mobile, Alabama, 107
Mockumentary, 87

145

Moderate, 99
Monterrey, 9
Montgomery, Alabama, 13, 29, 91
Monticello, 59, 60
Mother, 59
Mt. Sinai, 82
Murfreesboro, Tennessee, 67
Murphy J. Foster, 20
Myocardial infarction, 31

Narciso López, 10
Nashville Convention, 46, 107
Nashville, Tennessee, 107
Nassau, Bahamas, 85
Nazareth, Pennsylvania, 107
Nazi Germany, 87
New International Encyclopedia, 128, 130
New Jersey, 66
New Mexico, 46
New Orleans, Louisiana, 4, 9, 81
New Orleans Mint, 75
New South, 5
New York, 26
New York City, 26, 31
New York Times, 69
Norfolk, Virginia, 84, 114
Northampton County, North Carolina, 89
North Carolina, 81, 89
North Carolina Democratic Party, 90
North Carolina General Assembly, 89
Northeastern Mexico, 10
Northern United States, 64
Northern Virginia Campaign, 48
Norwich University, 89
Nueces River, 45
Nullification Crisis, 27, 74

Oakland Cemetery (Atlanta, Georgia), 41
Ocala, Florida, 85
Oconee Hill Cemetery, 31
Official Records of the American Civil War, 31
Ohio, 82
Open letter, 100
Oregon, 46
Origin of the Late War, 52
Orphan Brigade, 66

Pacific Railroad Surveys, 11
Palestine, Texas, 99
Paris, 49, 80, 81
Peace conference of 1861, 62, 94
Peculiar institution, 46
Peninsula Campaign, 29, 48
Pensacola, Florida, 105, 107
Père Lachaise Cemetery, 86, 87
P.G.T. Beauregard, 83

P. G. T. Beauregard, 13, 116
Phi Kappa Literary Society, 27, 35
Philip Francis Thomas, 26
Plain Folk of the Old South, 16
Plantation, 60, 81
Plantations in the American South, 6
Planter, 58, 83
Pocahontas, 59
Political figure, 94
Political leaders, 89
Political platform, 66
Politician, 4, 44, 56, 58, 61, 74, 77, 80, 89, 98, 105
Politics of the United States, 98
Pope Pius IX, 17
Popular sovereignty, 37
Popular vote, 64
Port Hudson, Louisiana, 67
Portland, Maine, 11
Postage stamps and postal history of the Confederate States, 12
Postmaster, 98
Practice of law, 65
Preface, 1
Presbyterian, 34, 56
Presbyterianism, 34
Presidency and the Civil War, 40
President of the Confederate States, 69, 90
President of the Confederate States of America, 3, 5
President of the United States, 5, 27, 36, 51, 59, 65
President pro tempore, 28
Princeton University, 64, 65
Prisoner of war, 29
Prisoner-of-war camp, 29
Probate court, 99
Project Gutenberg, 23, 49
Provisional Confederate Congress, 25, 62, 75, 94, 99
Pseudonym, 86
Public domain, 31, 54

Queens Counsel, 80, 87

Radical Republicans, 31
Railroad Commission of Texas, 101
Raleigh, North Carolina, 89, 90
Randolph-Macon College, 53
Reagan County, Texas, 102
Reason magazine, 128
Reconstruction Acts, 31
Reconstruction era, 86
Reconstruction era of the United States, 5, 31, 34, 101, 118
Reform Judaism, 81

Regent, 10
Republican Party (United States), 38, 64
Resolution (law), 66
Rice University, 21
Richard Howell, 8
Richard L. T. Beale, 50
Richmond and Danville Railroad, 16
Richmond Mechanics Institute, 59
Richmond, Virginia, 13, 62, 69, 100, 106
Rio Grande, 16, 45
Roanoke Island, 84
Robert Anderson (Civil War), 13
Robert Charles Winthrop, 25
Robert E. Lee, 5, 30, 52, 66, 67, 84, 85, 100
Robert H. Chilton, 9
Robert Jefferson Breckinridge, 66
Robert M. Charlton, 43
Robert Mercer Taliaferro Hunter, 15, 43, 79
Robert M. T. Hunter, **50**
Robert Skimin, 87
Robert Toombs, 13, 28, 36, 38, **43**, 51, 57, 75, 83, 99, 111
Robert Toombs Christian Academy, 49
Robert Toombs House, 49
Robert Woodward Barnwell, 25
Roger Lawson Gamble, 26
Roman Catholic, 81

Saint Croix, U.S. Virgin Islands, 80
Saint Francisville, Louisiana, 7
Sam Houston, 102
Samuel B. Maxey, 97
Samuel Chilton, 50
Sarah Knox Taylor, 4, 6
Savannah, Georgia, 39, 78
Schenectady, New York, 44
Seaborn Reese, 34
Secession, 29, 38, 46, 56, 66, 74, 98
Secession in the United States, 5
Secretary of the Navy, 110
Secretary of the Treasury, 29
Secret Six, 18
Seminole, 108
Sephardic, 80
Sephardic Jew, 80
Seven Days Battles, 29, 48
Sevier County, Tennessee, 98
Shelby Foote, 100
Shenandoah Valley, 67
Shermans March to the Sea, 30
Shreveport, Louisiana, 16
Siege, 9
Siege of Port Hudson, 64
Siege of Vicksburg, 100
Slavery, 28, 66
Slavery in the United States, 35

Sloops-of-war, 109
Smithsonian Institution, 10
Soldier, 4
South America, 18
South Carolina, 11, 74
Southern Democrat, 27
Southern United States, 56, 64, 66
Southern Victory Series, 87
Spar torpedo, 116
Speaker of the House, 51
Speaker of the United States House of Representatives, 25, 27, 50
SS George Davis, 94
SS Georgiana, 78
SS Robert M. T. Hunter, 52
Stafford County, Virginia, 61
State legislature (United States), 99
Statesman, 51
States rights, 10, 112
Stephen Adams (politician), 4
Stephen A. Douglas, 51
Stephen Douglas, 64
Stephen F. Austin, 102
Stephen Mallory, 14, 38, 47, 57, 75, 83, 99, **105**
Stephen Mallory II, 106
Stephen Russell Mallory, 119
Stephens County, Georgia, 41
Stevens Battery, 109
St. Louis Cathedral, 81
St. Mary Parish, Louisiana, 6
St. Rose Priory, 6
Sugar cane, 81
Supreme Court of the United States, 38
Surveying, 98

Taliaferro County, Georgia, 34
Tappahannock, Virginia, 52
Tariff of 1857, 51
Ten Commandments, 82
Tennessee, 66, 98
Texas, 9, 36, 45, 97–99
Texas A&M University, 18
Texass 1st congressional district, 99
Texas State Historical Association, 101
The Guns of the South, 87
Theophilus H. Holmes, 15
The Rise and Fall of the Confederate Government, 11
Thomas Bennett, Jr., 74
Thomas Bragg, 15, 80, **89**
Thomas Butler King, 26
Thomas D. Clark, 126
Thomas Flournoy Foster, 26
Thomas Hill Watts, 15
Thomas H. Watts, 89, **91**, 93

Thomas Jefferson, 58, 59
Thomas J. Jackson, 83
Thomas Mann Randolph Jr., 59
Thomas Reade Rootes Cobb, 27, 31
Thomas Stanley Bocock, 26
Thomas Willis Cobb, 31
Tilghman M. Tucker, 4
Toombs Bill, 46
Transylvania University, 4, 5, 64, 65
Treason, 5, 69
Treaty of Guadalupe Hidalgo, 10
Trinidad, 105, 107
Tuberculosis, 60

Ulysses S. Grant, 16
Union (American Civil War), 5, 29, 52, 56, 66, 98
Union Army, 16
Union College, 44
Union Springs, Alabama, 92
United Daughters of the Confederacy, 21
United Kingdom, 80, 84
United Kingdom of Great Britain and Ireland, 69
United States, 4, 5, 27, 38, 44, 51, 52, 55, 56, 58, 59, 61, 74, 77, 105
United States Ambassador to Spain, 65
United States Army, 4
United States Attorney General, 64
United States Congress, 51
United States Constitution, 10, 66
United States Democratic Party, 27, 35, 61, 98
United States Department of Transportation, 128
United States House of Representatives, 8, 26, 27, 34, 45, 50, 63, 64, 98, 106, 108
United States Military Academy, 4, 6
United States Mint, 75
United States Navy, 59
United States of America, 4
United States Post Office Department, 100
United States presidential election, 1844, 8
United States presidential election, 1860, 11, 64, 66
United States Secretary of State, 51, 111
United States Secretary of the Treasury, 26
United States Secretary of Treasury, 27
United States Secretary of War, 3, 5
United States Senate, 5, 36, 40, 45, 50, 51, 63, 64, 66, 90, 106, 108
United States Senate Committee on Armed Services, 10
United States Senate Committee on Claims, 90
United States Senator, 3, 43, 97, 106
United States Supreme Court, 80
United States Whig Party, 35, 45, 81

University of Georgia, 26, 27, 35, 44
University of North Carolina at Chapel Hill, 93, 94
University of South Carolina, 74
University of Virginia, 44, 51, 59, 62, 91
University of Virginia Law School, 44
USA.gov, 127
U.S. House Committee on Mileage, 27
U.S. House of Representatives, 4, 34, 97
U.S. President, 28, 59
U.S. presidential election, 1852, 10
U.S. presidential election, 1860, 47
USS Cairo (1861), 116
USS Congress (1841), 114
USS Cumberland (1842), 114
US Senate, 80
USS Housatonic (1861), 116
USS Merrimack (1855), 114, 132
USS Minnesota (1855), 114
USS Monitor, 114
USS New Ironsides, 116
U.S. state, 10, 89, 91, 98
U.S. Vice President, 28
U.S. Virgin Islands, 81

Vaihingen an der Enz, 73, 74
Valley Campaigns of 1864, 67
Varina Anne Davis, 9
Varina Davis, 66
Varina Howell, 4, 8
Varina Howell Davis, 86
Vice President, 34
Vice President of the Confederate States of America, 33
Vice President of the United States, 63, 64, 66
Virginia, 50, 51, 61, 74
Virginia Colony, 89
Virginia Historical Society, 59
Virginia House of Delegates, 51
Virginia Military Institute, 64, 67
Virginias 8th congressional district, 50
Virginias 9th congressional district, 50
Virginia (U.S. state), 64

Waldo, Florida, 17
Wales, 6
Walker Tariff, 46
Walter T. Colquitt, 26
War of 1812, 6, 31
Warren County, Mississippi, 7
Warrenton Academy, 89
Warrenton, North Carolina, 89
Washington County, Kentucky, 6
Washington, D.C., 39, 46, 59, 62, 67, 100
Washington, Georgia, 16, 44, 48, 85, 117
Washington, Mississippi, 6

148

Western Theater of the American Civil War, 13, 67
West Indies, 80
West Point, 5
Whig Party (United States), 34, 44, 51, 82
White House of the Confederacy, 13
Wilkes County, Georgia, 44
Wilkinson County, Mississippi, 6
William Alexander (American general), 61
William B. Preston, 59
William H. Martin, 97
William H. Seward, 13, 111
William Lowndes Yancey, 14
William Randolph, 59
William R. King, 10, 28, 63
William S. Archer, 50
William S. Herndon, 98
William T. Sherman, 29, 69
William T. Sutherlin, 17
William Whitaker (pioneer), 85
William Y. Thompson, 45, 128, 129
Willoughby Newton, 50
Wilmington, North Carolina, 93, 94
Wilmot Proviso, 36, 46
Wilsons Raid, 30
Wisconsin, 6
W. Patrick Lang, 87
Württemberg, 73, 74

Yale College, 80
Yale University, 81
Yellow fever, 9, 74

Zachary Taylor, 6, 25, 28, 36

www.ingramcontent.com/pod-product-compliance
Lightning Source LLC
Chambersburg PA
CBHW070554160426
43199CB00014B/2506